W9-BXF-948

Studs Terkel's WORKING

Adapted by HARVEY PEKAR

Edited by PAUL BUHLE

Studs Terkel's
WORKING

A Graphic Adaptation

WILLIAMSBURG REGIONAL LIBRARY
7770 CROAKER ROAD
WILLIAMSBURG, VIRGINIA 23188

MAY   2009

THE NEW PRESS

NEW YORK
LONDON

© 2009 by Harvey Pekar and Paul Buhle
Original introduction to *Working* © 1972, 1974 by Studs Terkel (originally published by
Pantheon Books)
All rights reserved.
No part of this book may be reproduced, in any form, without written permission from
the publisher.

Unless otherwise noted, all art is copyright their respective creators.

Requests for permission to reproduce selections from this book should be mailed to:
Permissions Department, The New Press, 38 Greene Street, New York, NY 10013.

Published in the United States by The New Press, New York, 2009
Distributed by Perseus Distribution

LIBRARY OF CONGRESS CATALOGING-IN-PUBLICATION DATA
Pekar, Harvey.
Studs Terkel's Working : a graphic adaptation / adapted by Harvey Pekar ;
edited by Paul Buhle.
     p. cm.
ISBN 978-1-59558-321-5 (pb)
1. Working class—United States—Pictorial works. 2. Working
class—United States—Interviews. 3. Working class—United
States—Attitudes. I. Buhle, Paul, 1944- II. Terkel, Studs, 1912-2008.
Working. III. Title.
 HD8072.T4 2009
 331.20973—dc22
                    2008047894

The New Press was established in 1990 as a not-for-profit alternative to the large, commercial publishing houses currently dominating the book publishing industry. The New
Press operates in the public interest rather than for private gain, and is committed to
publishing, in innovative ways, works of educational, cultural, and community value that
are often deemed insufficiently profitable.

www.thenewpress.com

Book design by Lovedog Studio
This book was set in Bodoni Book

Printed in the United States of America

10 9 8 7 6 5 4 3 2 1

Contents

Footwork

In the Spotlight

Behind a Desk

Appearance

Cleaning Up

Second Chance

Looking After Each Other
(From Cradle to Grave)

Preface

I was especially pleased to work on this project because Studs Terkel puts a great deal of emphasis, as I do, in writing about quotidian life. The so-called normal aspect of human existence is underemphasized in every form of literature, yet that is the aspect that most readers are familiar with and can most easily identify with.

The style of life I myself am familiar with is the quotidian.

But just because one writes about everyday life doesn't mean it's uninteresting; in fact, I find it's most fascinating, because it is so seldom written about. Virtually every person is potentially a great subject for a novel or a biography or a film. Bravo to Terkel for documenting these fascinating lives.

—*Harvey Pekar*

Acknowledgments

Our foremost thanks go naturally to the interviewees, to Studs, and to the artists and scriptwriters who contributed their work to this volume. My personal thanks go to assorted savants and friends, be it through teaching, research, or library work in the field of oral history—above all to Ron Grele, formerly director of the Oral History office at Columbia University, and to the staff at the Tamiment Library of New York University, where the Oral History of the American Left project that I launched in 1976 accommodated myself and the results of my work with great care and personal generosity. Thanks are also due to the editorial guidance of Marc Favreau and the painstaking work of Jason Ng.

—*Paul Buhle*

From the Original Introduction to Studs Terkel's WORKING

This book, being about work, is, by its very nature, about violence—to the spirit as well as to the body. It is about ulcers as well as accidents, about shouting matches as well as fistfights, about nervous breakdowns as well as kicking the dog around. It is, above all (or beneath all), about daily humiliations. To survive the day is triumph enough for the walking wounded among the great many of us.

The scars, psychic as well as physical, brought home to the supper table and the TV set, may have touched, malignantly, the soul of our society. More or less. ("More or less," that most ambiguous of phrases, pervades many of the conversations that comprise this book, reflecting, perhaps, an ambiguity of attitude toward The Job. Something more than Orwellian acceptance, something less than Luddite sabotage. Often the two impulses are fused in the same person.)

It is about a search, too, for daily meaning as well as daily bread, for recognition as well as cash, for astonishment rather than torpor; in short, for a sort of life rather than a Monday through Friday sort of dying. Perhaps immortality, too, is part of the quest. To be remembered was the wish, spoken and unspoken, of the heroes and heroines of this book.

There are, of course, the happy few who find a savor in their daily job: the Indiana stonemason, who looks upon his work and sees that it is good; the Chicago piano tuner, who seeks and finds the sound that delights; the bookbinder, who saves a piece of history; the Brooklyn fireman, who saves a piece of life. . . . But don't these satisfactions, like Jude's hunger for knowledge, tell us more about the person than about his task? Perhaps. Nonetheless, there is a common attribute here: a meaning to their work well over and beyond the reward of the paycheck.

For the many, there is a hardly concealed discontent. The blue-collar blues is no more bitterly sung than the white-collar moan. "I'm a machine," says the spot-welder. "I'm caged," says the bank teller, and echoes the hotel clerk. "I'm a mule," says the steelworker. "A monkey can do what I do," says the receptionist. "I'm less than a farm implement," says the migrant worker. "I'm an object," says the high-fashion model. Blue collar and white call upon the identical phrase: "I'm a robot." *There is nothing to talk about,* the young accountant despairingly enunciates. It was some time ago that John Henry sang, "A man ain't nothin' but a man." The hard, unromantic fact is: he died with his hammer in his hand, while the machine pumped on. Nonetheless, he found immortality. He is remembered.

As the automated pace of our daily jobs wipes out name and face—and, in many instances, feeling—there is a sacrilegious question being asked these days. To earn one's bread by the sweat of one's brow has always been the lot of mankind. At least, ever since Eden's slothful couple was served with an eviction notice. The scriptural precept was never doubted, not out loud. No matter how demeaning the task, no matter how it dulls the senses and breaks the spirit, one *must* work. Or else.

Lately there has been a questioning of this "work ethic," especially by the young. Strangely enough, it has touched off profound grievances in others, hithero devout, silent, and anonymous. Unexpected precincts are being heard from in a show of discontent. Communiqués from the assembly line are frequent and alarming: absenteeism. On the evening bus, the tense, pinched faces of young file clerks and elderly secretaries tell us more than we care to know. On the expressways, middle management men pose without grace behind their wheels as they flee city and job.

There are other means of showing it, too. Inchoately, sullenly, it appears in slovenly work, in the put-down of craftsmanship. A farm equipment worker in Moline complains that the careless worker who turns out more that is bad is better regarded than the careful craftsman who turns out less that is good. The first is an ally of the Gross National Product. The other is a threat to it, a kook—and the sooner he is penalized the better. Why, in these circumstances, should a man work with care? Pride does indeed precede the fall.

Others, more articulate—at times, visionary—murmur of a hunger for "beauty," "a meaning," "a sense of pride." A veteran car hiker sings out, "I could drive any car like a baby, like a woman change her baby's diaper. Lots of customers say, 'How you do this?' I'd say, 'Just the way you bake a cake, miss.' When I was younger, I could swing with that car. They called me Lovin' Al the Wizard."

Dolores Dante graphically describes the trials of a waitress in a fashionable restaurant. They are compounded by her refusal to be demeaned. Yet pride in her skills helps her make it through the night. "When I put the plate down, you don't hear a sound. When I pick up a glass, I want it to be just right. When someone says, 'How come you're just a waitress?' I say, 'Don't you think you deserve being served by me?'"

Peggy Terry has her own sense of grace and beauty. Her jobs have varied with geography, climate, and the ever-felt pinch of circumstance. "What I hated worst was being a waitress. The way you're treated. One guy said, 'You don't have to smile; I'm gonna give you a tip anyway.' I said, 'Keep it. I wasn't smiling for a tip.' Tipping should be done away with. It's like throwing a dog a bone. It makes you feel small."

In all instances, there is felt more than a slight ache. In all instances, there dangles the impertinent question: Ought not there be an increment, earned though not yet received, from one's daily work—an acknowledgment of man's *being*?

An American president is fortunate—or, perhaps, unfortunate—that, offering his Labor Day homily, he didn't encounter Maggie Holmes, the domestic, or Phil Stallings, the spot-welder, or Louis Hayward, the washroom attendant. Or, especially, Grace Clements, the felter at the luggage factory, whose daily chore reveals to us in a terrible light that Charles Dickens's London is not so far away nor long ago.

Obtuseness in "respectable" quarters is not a new phenomenon. In 1850 Henry Mayhew, digging deep into London's laboring lives and evoking from the invisible people themselves the wretched truth of their lot, astonished and horrified readers of the *Morning Chronicle*. His letters ran six full columns and averaged 10,500 words. It is inconceivable that Thomas Carlyle was unaware of Mayhew's findings. Yet, in his usual acerbic—and, in this instance, unusually mindless—manner, he blimped, "No needlewoman, distressed or other, can be procured in London by any housewife to give, for fair wages, fair help in sewing. Ask any thrifty housemother. No *real* needlewoman, 'distressed' or other, has been found attainable in any of the houses I frequent. Imaginary needlewomen, who demand considerable wages, and have a deepish appetite for beer and viands, I hear of everywhere. . . .* A familiar ring?

Smug respectability, like the poor, we've had with us always. Today, however, and what few decades remain of the twentieth century, such obtuseness is an indulgence we can no longer afford. The computer, nuclear energy for better or worse, and sudden, simultaneous influences flashed upon everybody's TV screen have raised the ante and the risk considerably. Possibilities of another way, discerned by only a few before, are thought of—if only for a brief moment, in the haze of idle conjecture—by many today.

The drones are no longer invisible nor mute. Nor are they exclusively of one class. Markham's Man with the Hoe may be Ma Bell's girl with the headset. (And can it be safely said she is "dead to rapture and despair"? Is she really "a thing that grieves not and that never hopes"?) They're in the office as well as the warehouse; at the manager's desk as well as the assembly line;

*E.P. Thompson and Eileen Yeo, eds., *The Unknown Mayhew* (New York: Pantheon Books, 1971).

at some estranged company's computer as well as some estranged woman's kitchen floor.

Bob Cratchit may still be hanging on (though his time is fast running out, as did his feather pen long ago), but Scrooge has been replaced by the conglomerate. Hardly a chance for Christmas spirit here. Who knows Bob's name in this outfit—let alone his lame child's? ("The last place I worked for, I was let go," recalls the bank teller. "One of my friends stopped by and asked where I was at. They said, 'She's no longer with us.' That's all. I vanished.") It's nothing personal, really. Dickens's people have been replaced by Beckett's.

> Many old working class women have an habitual gesture which illuminates the years of their life behind. D.H. Lawrence remarked it in his mother: my grandmother's was a repeated tapping which accompanied an endless working out of something in her head; she had years of making out for a large number on very little. In others, you see a rhythmic smoothing out of the hand down the chair arm, as though to smooth everything out and make it workable; in others, there is a working of the lips or a steady rocking. None of these could be called neurotic gestures, nor are they symptoms of acute fear; they help the constant calculation.*

In my mother's case, I remember the illuminating gesture associated with work or enterprise. She was a small entrepreneur, a Mother Courage fighting her Thirty Years' War daily. I remember her constant feeling of the tablecloth, as though assessing its quality, and her squinting of the eye, as though calculating its worth.

Perhaps it was myopia, but I rarely saw such signs among the people I visited during this adventure. True, in that dark hollow in Eastern Kentucky I did see Susie Haynes, the black lung miner's wife, posed in the doorway of the shack, constantly touching the woodwork, "as though to smooth everything out and make it workable." It was a rare gesture, what once had been commonplace. Those who did signify—Ned Williams, the old stock chaser; Hobart Foote, the utility man—did so in the manner of the machines to which they were bound. Among the many, though the words and phrases came, some heatedly, others coolly, the hands were at rest, motionless. Their eyes were something else again. As they talked of their jobs, it was as though it had little to do with their felt lives. It was an alien matter. At times I imagined I was on the estate of Dr. Caligari and the guests poured out fantasies.

––––

*Richard Hoggart, *The Uses of Literacy* (New York: Oxford University Press, 1957).

To maintain a sense of self, these heroes and heroines play occasional games. The middle-aged switchboard operator, when things are dead at night, cheerily responds to the caller, "Marriott Inn," instead of identifying the motel chain she works for. "Just for a lark," she explains bewilderedly. "I really don't know what made me do it." The young gas meter reader startles the young suburban housewife sunning out on the patio in her bikini, loose-bra'd, and sees more things than he would otherwise see. "Just to make the day go faster." The auto worker from the Deep South will "tease one guy 'cause he's real short and his old lady left him." Why? "Oh, just to break the monotony. You want quittin' time so bad."

The waitress, who moves by the tables with the grace of a ballerina, pretends she's forever on stage. "I feel like Carmen. It's like a gypsy holding out a tambourine and they throw the coin." It helps her fight humiliation as well as arthritis. The interstate truck driver, bearing down the expressway with a load of seventy-three thousand pounds, battling pollution, noise, an ulcer, and kidneys that act up, "fantasizes something tremendous." They all, in some manner, perform astonishingly to survive the day. These are not yet automata.

The time study men of the General Motors Assembly Division made this discomfiting discovery in Lordstown. Gary Bryner, the young union leader, explains it. "Occasionally one of the guys will let a car go by. At that point, he's made a decision: 'Aw, fuck it. It's only a car.' It's more important to just stand there and rap. With us, it becomes a human thing. It's the most enjoyable part of my job, that moment. I love it!" John Henry hardly envisioned that way of fighting the machine—which may explain why he died in his prime.

There are cases where the job possesses the man even after quitting time. Aside from occupational ticks of hourly workers and the fitful sleep of salaried ones, there are instances of a man's singular preoccupation with work. It may affect his attitude toward all of life. And art.

Geraldine Page, the actress, recalls the critique of a backstage visitor during her run in *Sweet Bird of Youth*. He was a dentist. "I was sitting in the front row and looking up. Most of the time I was studying the fillings in your mouth. I'm curious to know who's been doing your dental work." It was not that he loved theater less, but that he loved dentistry more.

At the public unveiling of a celebrated statue in Chicago, a lawyer, after deep study, mused, "I accept Mr. Picasso in good faith. But if you look at the height of the slope on top and the propensity of children who will play on it, I have a feeling that some child may fall and be hurt and the county may be sued. . . ."

In my own case, while putting together this book, I found myself possessed by the mystique of work. During a time out, I saw the film *Last Tango in Paris*. Though Freud said *lieben und arbeiten* are the two moving impulses of man, it was the latter that, at the moment, consumed me.* Thus, I saw on the screen a study not of redemption nor of self-discovery nor whatever perceptive critics may have seen. During that preoccupied moment I saw a study of an actor *at work*. He was performing brilliantly in a darkened theater (apartment), as his audience (the young actress) responded with enthusiasm. I interpreted her moans, cries, and whimpers as bravos, huzzahs, and olés. In short, I saw the film as a source of a possible profile for this book. Such is the impact of work on some people.

A further personal note. I find some delight in my job as a radio broadcaster. I'm able to set my own pace, my own standards, and determine for myself the substance of each program. Some days are more sunny than others, some hours less astonishing than I'd hoped for; my occasional slovenliness infuriates me . . . but it is, for better or worse, in my hands. I'd like to believe I'm the old-time cobbler, making the whole shoe. Though my weekends go by soon enough, I look toward Monday without a sigh.

The danger of complacency is somewhat tempered by my awareness of what might have been. Chance encounters with old schoolmates are sobering experiences. Memories are dredged up of three traumatic years at law school. They were vaguely, though profoundly, unhappy times for me. I felt more than a slight ache. Were it not for a fortuitous set of circumstances, I might have become a lawyer—a determinedly failed one, I suspect. (I flunked my first bar examination. Ninety percent passed, I was told.)

During the Depression I was a sometime member of the Federal Writers' Project, as well as a sometime actor in radio soap operas. I was usually cast as a gangster and just as usually came to a violent and well-deserved end. It was always sudden. My tenure was as uncertain as that of a radical college professor. It was during these moments—though I was unaware of it at the time—that the surreal nature of my work made itself felt. With script in hand, I read lines of stunning banality. The more such scripts an actor read, the more he was considered a success. Thus the phrase "Show Business" took on an added significance. It was, indeed, a business, a busyness. But what was its meaning?

If Freud is right—"his work at least gives him a secure place in a portion of reality, in the human community"*—was what I did in those studios really work? It certainly wasn't play. The sales charts of Proctor & Gamble

*Sigmund Freud, *Civilization and Its Discontents* (New York: W.W. Norton and Co., 1962).

and General Mills made that quite clear. It was considered *work*. All my colleagues were serious about it, deadly so. Perhaps my experiences in making life difficult for Ma Perkins and Mary Marlin may have provided me with a metaphor for the experiences of the great many, who fail to find in their work their "portion of reality." Let alone, a secure place "in the human community."

Is it any wonder that in such surreal circumstances, status rather than the work itself becomes important? Thus the prevalence of euphemisms in work as well as in war. The janitor is a building engineer; the garbage man, a sanitary engineer; the man at the rendering plant, a factory mechanic; the gravedigger, a caretaker. They are not themselves ashamed of their work, but society, they feel, looks upon them as a lesser species. So they call upon a promiscuously used language to match the "respectability" of others, whose jobs may have less social worth than their own.

(The airline stewardess understands this hierarchy of values. "When you first start flying . . . the men you meet are airport employees: ramp rats, cleaning airplanes and things like that, mechanics. . . . After a year we get tired of that, so we move into the city to get involved with men that are usually young executives. . . . They wear their hats and their suits and in the winter their black gloves.")

Not that these young men in white shirts and black gloves are so secure, either. The salesman at the advertising agency is an account executive. "I feel a little downgraded if people think I'm a salesman. Account executive—that describes my job. It has more prestige than just saying, 'I'm a salesman.'" A title, like clothes, may not make the man or woman, but it helps in the world of peers—and certainly impresses strangers. "We're all vice presidents," laughs the copy chief. "Clients like to deal with vice presidents. Also, it's a cheap thing to give somebody. Vice presidents get fired with great energy and alacrity."

At hospitals, the charming bill collector is called the patients' representative! It's a wonderland that Alice never envisioned. Consider the company spy. With understandable modesty, he refers to himself as an industrial investigator. This last—under the generic name, Security—is among the most promising occupations in our society today. No matter how tight the job market, here is a burgeoning field for young men and women. Watergate, its magic spell is everywhere.

In a further bizarre turn of events (the science of medicine has increased our life expectancy; the science of business frowns upon the elderly), the matter of age is felt in almost all quarters. "Thirty and out" is the escape hatch for the elderly autoworker to the woods of retirement, some hunting, some fishing. . . . But thirty has an altogether different connotation at the ad agency, at the bank, at the auditing house, at the gas company. Unless he/she is "with it" by then, it's out to the woods of the city, some hunting, some fishing of another sort. As the workforce becomes increasingly younger, so does Willy Loman. [. . .]

Perhaps it is time the "work ethic" was redefined and its idea reclaimed from the banal men who invoke it. In a world of cybernetics, of an almost runaway technology, things are increasingly making things. It is for our species, it would seem, to go on to other matters. Human matters. Freud put it one way. Ralph Helstein puts it another. He is president emeritus of the United Packinghouse Workers of America. "Learning is work. Caring for children is work. Community action is work. Once we accept the concept of work as something meaningful—not just as the source of a buck—you don't have to worry about finding enough jobs. There's no excuse for mules any more. Society does not need them. There's no question about our ability to feed and clothe and house everybody. The problem is going to come in finding enough ways for man to keep occupied, so he's in touch with reality." Our imaginations have obviously not yet been challenged.

"It isn't that the average working guy is dumb. He's tired, that's all." Mike LeFevre, the steelworker, asks rhetorically, "Who you gonna sock? You can't sock General Motors . . . you can't sock a system." So, at the neighborhood tavern, he socks the patron sitting next to him, the average working guy. And look out below! It's predetermined, his work being what it is.

"Even a writer as astringent and seemingly unromantic as Orwell never quite lost the habit of seeing working classes through the cozy fug of an Edwardian music hall. There is a wide range of similar attitudes running down through the folksy ballyhoo of the Sunday columnists, the journalists who always remember with admiration the latest bon mot of their pub pal, 'Alf.'"*

Similarly, on our shores, the myth dies hard. The most perdurable and certainly the most dreary is that of the cabdriver-philosopher. Our columnists still insist on citing him as the perceptive "diamond in the rough" social observer. Lucky Miller, a young cabdriver, has his say in this matter. "A lot of drivers, they'll agree to almost anything the passenger will say, no matter how absurd. They're angling for that tip." Barbers and bartenders are probably not far behind as being eminently quotable. They are also tippable. This in no way reflects on the nature of their work so much as on the slothfulness of journalists, and the phenomenon of tipping. "Usually I do not disagree with a customer," says a barber. "That's gonna hurt business." It's predetermined, his business—or work—being what it is.

Simultaneously, as our "Alf," called "Archie" or "Joe," is romanticized, he is caricatured. He is the clod, put down by others. The others, who call

*Richard Hoggart, *The Uses of Literacy.*

themselves middle-class, are in turn put down by still others, impersonal in nature—The Organization, The Institution, The Bureaucracy. "Who you gonna sock? You can't sock General Motors . . ." Thus the "dumbness" (or numbness or tiredness) of both classes is encouraged and exploited in a society more conspicuously manipulative than Orwell's. A perverse alchemy is at work: the gold that may be found in their unexamined lives is transmuted into the dross of banal being. This put-down and its acceptance have been made possible by a perverted "work ethic."

But there are stirrings, a nascent flailing about. Though "Smile" buttons appear, the bearers are deadpan because nobody smiles back. What with the computer and all manner of automation, new heroes and antiheroes have been added to Walt Whitman's old work anthem. The sound is no longer melodious. The desperation is unquiet.

Nora Watson may have said it most succinctly. "I think most of us are looking for a calling, not a job. Most of us, like the assembly-line worker, have jobs that are too small for our spirit. Jobs are not big enough for people."

During my three years of prospecting, I may have, on more occasions than I had imagined, struck gold. I was constantly astonished by the extraordinary dreams of ordinary people. No matter how bewildering the times, no matter how dissembling the official language, those we call ordinary are aware of a sense of personal worth—or more often a lack of it—in the work they do. Tom Patrick, the Brooklyn fireman whose reflections end the book, similarly brings this essay to a close:

"The fuckin' world's so fucked up, the country's fucked up. But the firemen, you actually see them produce. You see them put out a fire. You see them come out with babies in their hands. You see them give mouth-to-mouth when a guy's dying. You can't get around that shit. That's real. To me, that's what I want to be.

"I worked in a bank. You know, it's just paper. It's not real. Nine to five and it's shit. You're lookin' at numbers. But I can look back and say, 'I helped put out a fire. I helped save somebody.' It shows something I did on this earth."

Introduction

The work of Studs Terkel has been "visual" from the beginning, and a comic art book based upon a selection of his interviews in the totemic oral history volume *Working* would seem the natural extension of his essential impulses. Terkel's interviewing has found a counterpart, for the last thirty years or so, in the comics scripted by Harvey Pekar. The two are joined here, adapted by a dozen talented artists, in what we believe to be a fresh approach to the lives and labor of ordinary Americans. It will also mark the maturity of comic art, now recognized as a distinctive American art form.

File clerk in the Cleveland Veterans Administration offices from 1966 until his 2001 retirement, Pekar has gone far to create, with his chosen artists, an art form hardly less intimate than Terkel's, with one marked contrast. Studs writes about his life at length in the 2007 volume *Touch and Go*—that is, only after spending much of his career writing about others. Pekar, on the other hand, *started* with his own immediate experiences and worked outward toward friends, lovers, neighborhood, and society. Some critics would say that Pekar's work is the forerunner of the acclaimed nonfiction comics now running the gamut from Marjane Satrapi's *Persepolis* and Joe Sacco's *Palestine* and *Safe Area Gorazde* to Alison Bechdel's *Fun Home,* and some of the artists themselves cheerfully agree with this estimation. Pekar has helped expand readers' (and critics') understanding of what comics could be and what they could express. His work is absolutely crucial for the tradition in which this project belongs.

Still, a volume of comic art based upon a totemic oral history of American life and experience is an experiment, and our understanding must be rooted first of all in Studs Terkel's accomplishments. Every teacher of oral history knows that Terkel is the sole celebrity of a field dominated by the "amateur" work of nonprofessors, including documentary film-makers, community history enthusiasts, and others who lack PhDs but make up for this supposed limitation in their attention to the subject at hand.

Oral history itself has a highly curious history bound more closely to the visual than most readers would likely imagine. Before the printed word, nothing but oral history existed, and history was unraveled by individual and collective tale-tellers generation after generation in stories of creation and change. The poet Erza Pound occasionally reminded his readers that these primal stories were often told through dance and song, which were every bit as important as the words. If comics can be traced ultimately to cave-wall painting and its representation of past events or hoped-for events, then artist and poet could not have been far apart.

Oral history received a kind of modern jump start in the Works Progress Administration that is so much part of Studs Terkel's own life experience. There, in the New Deal years, the opportunity opened for government funding of extensive life-story interviews with aging African Americans who had grown up as slaves—the final opportunity to grasp this horrendous but all-important tale. The interviews were taken down in writing rather than taped, and often enough by descendents of slave-owners or other whites to whom ex-slaves were not likely to tell the unvarnished story. Still, the archives bulged with enough for nearly twenty volumes that finally, with the rise of Black history in the 1960s, found their way into print.

The next phase in the institutionalized development of oral history is remarkably different and equally revealing. The creation of a first presidential library with an oral history component, the Truman Library, found experts interviewing former officials, then carefully sending the transcripts to interviewees for "corrections," and even more carefully erasing, as per agreement, the original tapes. Nothing embarrassing could be revealed, although there was a lot to be embarrassed about in the business and political dealings of the first Cold War president and sworn enemy of Studs Terkel's all-time favorite political figure, the banished and red-baited former vice president Henry Wallace. The earliest oral history project to achieve wide distinction for a more general approach was established by Allen Nevins at Columbia in 1948 and with a related if less disingenuous purpose: to preserve the life stories of important men who had failed to write memoirs.

What happened next in the field of oral history was Terkelesque for the reason that it was owed enormously, if by no means entirely, to Terkel. By the time an oral history association was founded by academics and others, the 1960s was under way. The generation that swept into oral history was more than deeply influenced by the movements for civil rights, peace, and gender-liberation: the oral historians were themselves very often part of these movements. *Working*, as Terkel has often said, began with the oral historian's decades in radio, but also with Pantheon editor Andre Schiffrin's urgings, based in no small measure on Schiffrin's own political past and commitments. The volumes that followed in Terkel's career can be seen as a narrative of the "Other America," the one that had seemed invisible or unacceptable. What was true in the United States was even more true in Britain, where oral history had arisen close to socialistic legacies and sought to prompt long-standing blue collar communities to create and distribute their own collective tales.

Comics, meanwhile, had undergone several revolutions. The most important may have been a counterrevolution: the suppression of comic books, good and bad alike, in the mid-1950s, after Red Scare–style congressional hearings. Those comic books had more readers than the consumers of radio, television, and magazine altogether. They included, along with a large volume of dreck, searingly realistic stories, including antiwar narratives and the most serious kind of social commentary in the form of EC Comics (and their child, *Mad Comics*, later to become *Mad Magazine*).

In the generations following 1970, these scholarly, semischolarly, political, and artistic forms danced around each other and took on fresh meanings. Harvey Pekar, with the first issues of *American Splendor*, emerged only a few years after the publication of *Working* in a setting of a blue collar city, Cleveland, that could easily have been Chicago. Their parallel is something to ponder.

Now, in retrospect, the proximity has become a great deal more obvious. The eye for detail and individual observation, often quirky but always full of humanity, marks the Terkel–Pekar similarity most of all. It would be interesting to know if Terkel's theatrical experience is a precursor toward this degree of narrative wisdom, a disinclination to talk down to the audience even while lifting it up. The WPA theater and the avant-garde theater of the 1930s Left found Terkel, or he found it. Here, in the vicinity of a stylized but entirely original Clifford Odets's *Waiting for Lefty*, may have been a birthplace of Terkel's formal art, or at least his preparation for writing theatrical and radio drama. So much fell away with the post–World War II shutdown of American culture, but not everything. Even in the blacklist days, something survived.

Pekar and the other comic artists in this volume are children of different generations. The eldest were born toward the beginning of the 1940s, the youngest in the 1980s; but whether their past lies in writing *Spider-Man* or drawing a comic biography of Isadora Duncan, it is fair to say that they share a certain sensibility. They are egalitarians, eager to make the most of the details in Terkel's text, not only from personal predilection or political motive, but because these details best serve the art of the comic—an art evolving, like oral history, toward a future that never ceases to reflect a distant past in the common human saga.

—Paul Buhle
January 2009

Working the Land

Aunt Katherine's nephew and his wife. On this morning, a piece of sun peers over the Cumberlands. His speech comes with difficulty, due to partial paralysis on his face and shortage of breath. Frequently during the conversation we take time out. He wears a hearing aid.

Minin's about all the work here, outside highway work or farmin' a little. My father started workin' in the mines when he was eleven years old.

I guess he was fifty-seven when he quit, he had to. He had to walk across the big mountain and it'd be late into the night when he'd come back.

So we never got to see Daddy but on Sunday.

I graduated from high school in 1930, November. I went to work in the mines. We worked for fifteen cents a ton. If we made a dollar and a half a day, we made good money. You got up between three thirty and four in the morning. We usually got out around maybe dark or seven or eight, nine o'clock. I come back as late ten o'clock.
I got short winded and just couldn't walk across the street. The doctor advised me to quit work. My heart got bad to where I couldn't even get oxygen. March of '68 I quit. They turned me down for black lung. I'm paid through Social Security.

My hearin'... It coulda been affected with so much noise. I was tampin' up, shooting the coal down just behind the machine. That made lotsa noise. This hearin' aid cost me $395. I think the United Mine Workers has let us down a little bit. They teamed up with the operators, I think.

I went to school with a boy and he got mashed up in the mines. He was about eighteen years old when he got killed.

Oh, I remember lots of accidents. I guess there was eight or nine men killed while I worked at one. These truck mines I worked in was all. They wasn't union mines. The strip and auger about got 'em all shut down right now.

I have a nephew of mine run a mine. He worked about seventeen men. They all gone to unemployment now.

UNEMPLOYMENT OFFICE

You're in one of the richest areas in the world and some of the poorest people in the world. They's about twenty-eight gas and oil wells. They have one here they claim at least a three-million-dollar-a-year gas well. One of the men that works for the gas company said they valued it at twenty-five million dollars, that one well. They offered a woman seventy-five dollars an acre on the farm that the gas well's just laid on, for destroyin' half an acre of her place to set that well on.

You sold it to them for how much...Do you know what that land's worth?

You think I shouldna done it?

They can do that legally because they have the mineral rights. Eighteen eighty-nine, my grandfather sold this, everything known and all that might be found later... My grandfather and grandmother signed it with two X's. They accepted the farmin' rights. Company can dig all your timber, all your soil off, uncover everything. Go anywhere they want to, drill right in your garden if they want to.

They took bulldozers and they tore the top off the ground. I couldn't plow it or nothin' where they left it. I've got corn this year, first year I raised it. Nice corn over there. I had to move a lot of rock where they took the bulldozers.

They threatened my wife with trespassin' here because she called up the water pollution man, the gas and oil company did.

When they come through with them bulldozers and tear it up like that, the dirt runs to our bottom land and our drinkin' water gets muddy. So we don't have much of a chance, don't look like.

Our boy in the Navy when he comes back, he says all he can see is the mountain tore up with bulldozers. Even the new roads they built, they's debris on it and you can't hardly get through it sometimes.

What's the use of goin' over there and fightin' and then havin' to come back over here an' pay taxes on somethin' that's torn up like that?

It don't make sense, wrecking the land like this.

I guess that's what they sent our boys off to fight for, to keep 'em a free country and then they do to us like that. Nothin' we can do about it. He said it was worse here than it was over in Vietnam. Four times he been in Vietnam. He said this was a worse tore up place than Vietnam.

7

If we don't organize together why these big companies is just gonna take anything they want. That's the only chance on earth we got. It's all gone over to the rich man. Even the President. And we don't have a governor.

Everybody talk about it all the time. Especially Aunt Katherine up here, that's all me an' her talk about -- what they done to us. My mother and father sold all their land out, where my mother's buried. Company said they sold the mineral to some other company and they was goin' to auger it. We're not gonna let it happen to my mother's grave because there's seven of us children and I know that five of us will stay right there and see that they don't do that.

They said we'd get a road up to the cemetery that's on top of the hill. I said, "Well, it won't be any use goin' up there, because there won't be any dead up there. There'll just be tombstones settin' there. Because the coal is under the graves." An old preacher down there, they augered under the grave where his wife is buried.

It's something to think about, that a man to make a few dollars would go through and under a cemetery like that. Not even respecting the dead. You can't talk to 'em. They won't talk to you about it. They walk off and leave you.

Our son just came back from Vietnam, he went to work for a strip mine. We told him we wouldn't allow him to work for them and stay home. So he quit. He was tellin' me yesterday, looks like he's gonna have to go back to work.

I can't hold out no longer, Ma.

Well, do you want me to pack your clothes tonight or do you want to wait until morning to get 'em? 'Cause when you start workin' for the strip mines, you're not comin' back here. I'm not responsible for anything that happens to ya.

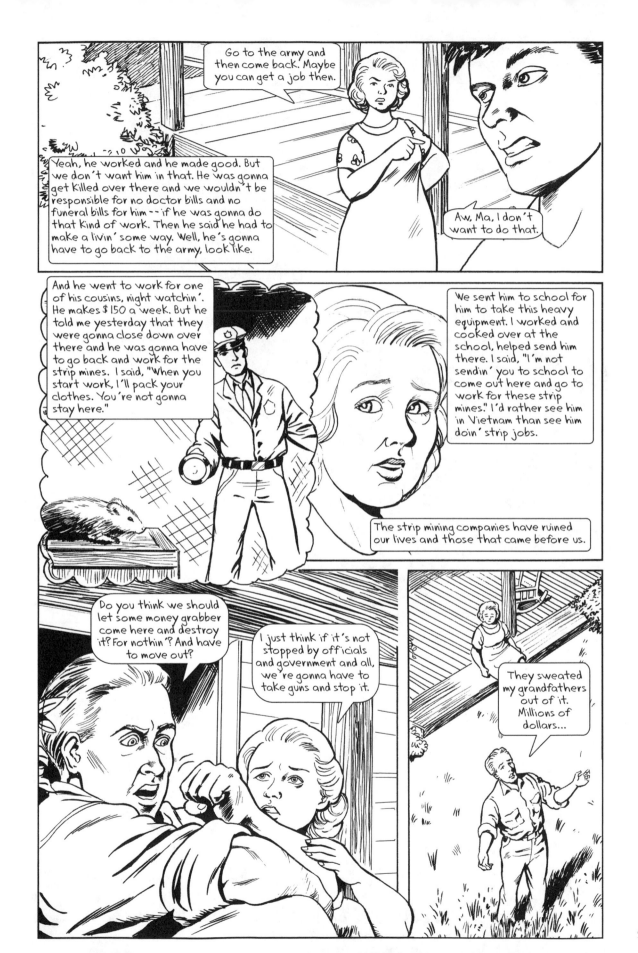

roberto acuna

FARMWORKER

by DYLAN A.T. MINER

I walked out of the fields two years ago. I saw the need to change the California feudal system, to change the lives of farm workers, to make these huge corporations feel they're not above anybody. I am thirty-four years old and I try to organize for the United Farmworkers of America.

His hands are calloused and each of his thumbnails is singularly cut. "If you're picking lettuce, the thumbnails fall off cause they're banged on the box. Your hands get swollen. You can't slow down because the foreman sees you're so many boxes behind and you'd better get on. But people would help each other. If you're feeling bad that day, somebody who's feeling pretty good would help. Any people that are suffering have to stick together, whether they like it or not, whether they be black, brown or pink."

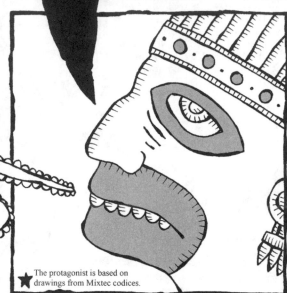

The protagonist is based on drawings from Mixtec codices.

According to Mom I was born on a cotton sack out in the fields 'cause she had no money to go to the hospital. When I was a child, we used to migrate from California to Arizona and back and forth. The things I saw shaped my life. I remember when we used to go out and pick carrots and onions, the whole family. We tried to scratch a livin' out of the ground. I saw my parents cry out in despair, even though we had the whole family working. At the time they were paying sixty two and a half cents an hour. The average income must have been fifteen hundred dollars, maybe two thousand.

This was supplemented by child labor. During these years the growers used to have a Pick-Your-Harvest week. They would get all the migrant kids out of school and have 'em out there pickin' the crops at peak harvest time. A child was off that week and when he came back to school he got a little gold star that would make it seem like something civic to do. We'd pick everything: lettuce, carrots, onions, cucumbers, cauliflower, broccoli, tomatoes- all the salads you could make out of vegetables, we picked 'em. We'd be in Salinas about four months. From there we'd go down into the Imperial Valley. From there we'd go to picking citrus. It was like a cycle. We'd follow the seasons.

After my dad died, my mom would come home and she'd go into her tent and I would go into ours. We'd roughhouse and everything and we'd go into the tent where mom was sleeping and I'd see her crying. When I asked her why she was crying she never gave me an answer; she said things would get better. She retired a beaten old lady with a lot of dignity. That day she thought would be better never came for her.

One time my mom was in bad need of money. So she got a part-time evening job in a restaurant. All the growers would come in and they'd be laughing makin' passes at her, makin' nasty remarks. I used to go out there and kick 'em and my mom told me to leave 'em alone; she could handle 'em. But they would embarrass her and she would cry.

CHEESY CRAFT!

(WHITE) RICH

POOR (MEXICANS)

My mom couldn't speak English too good. Or much Spanish for that matter. But she knew some prayers and she used to make us say them. That's another thing: when I see the many things in this world and this country, I could tear the churches apart. I never saw a priest out in the fields trying to help people. Maybe in these later years they're doing it. But it's always the church taking from the people. We were asked once by the church to bring vegetables to make it a successful bazaar. After we got the stuff there, the only people havin' a good time were the rich people, because they were the only ones that were buyin' stuff.

I'd go to school barefoot. The bad thing was they used to laugh at us, the Anglo kids. They would laugh because we'd bring tortillas and frijoles to lunch. They would have their nice little compact lunch boxes with cold milk in their thermos and they'd laugh at us because all we had were dried tortillas. Not only would they laugh at us, but kids would pick fights. My older brother used to do most of the fighting for us and he'd come home with black eyes all the time. What really hurt is when we had to go on welfare. Nobody knows the erosion of man's dignity. They used to have a label of canned goods that said, "U.S. Commodities Not to be sold or exchanged." Nobody knows how proud it is to feel when you bought canned goods with your money.

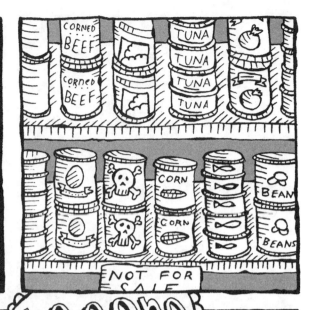

I wanted to be accepted. It must have been in the sixth grade. It was just before the Fourth of July. They were trying out students for this patriotic play. I wanted to do Abe Lincoln, so I learned the Gettysburg Address inside & out. I'd be in the fields pickin' the crops & I'd be memorizin'. I was the only one who didn't have to read the part 'cause I memorized it. The part was given to a girl who was a grower's daughter. She had to read it out of a book, but they said she had better diction. I was very disappointed. I quit about eigth grade. Anytime anybody'd talk to me about politics, about civil rights, I would ignore it. It's a very degrading thing because you can't express yourself. They wanted us to speak English in the school classes. We'd put out a real effort. I would get into a lot of fights because I spoke Spanish & they couldn't understand it. I was punished. I was kept after school for not speaking English.

We used to have our own tents on the truck. Most migrants would live in tents that were already there, in the fields, put up by the company. We got one for ourselves, second hand but it was ours—Anglos used to laugh at us. "Here comes the carnival," they'd say. We couldn't keep our clothes clean. We couldn't keep nothing clean because we'd go by the dirt roads and dust. We'd stay outside the town. I never did want to go to town because it was a bad thing for me. We used to go into small stores, even though we got clipped more. If we went to the other stores they would laugh at us. They would always point at us with a finger. We'd go to town maybe every two weeks to get what we needed. Everyone would walk in a bunch. We were afraid (laughs). We sang to keep our spirits up. We joked about our poverty. This one guy would say, "When I get to be rich, I'm gonna marry an Anglo woman, so I can be accepted into society." The other guy would say, "When I get rich I'm gonna marry a Mexican woman, so I can get to that Anglo society of yours and see them hang you for marrying an Anglo." Our world was around the fields.

I started picking crops when I was eight. I couldn't do much, but every little bit counts. Everytime I would get behind in my chores, I would get a carrot thrown at me by my parents. I would daydream: if I were a millionaire, I would buy all these ranches and give them back to the people. I would picture my mom living in one area all the time and being admired by all the people in the community. All of a sudden I'd be rudely awakened by a broken carrot in my back. That would bust your whole dream apart and you'd work for a while and come back daydreaming.

We used to work early, about four o'clock in the morning. We'd pick the harvest until about six. Then we'd run home and get into supposedly clean clothes and run all the way to school because we'd be late. By the time we got to school we'd be all tuckered out. Around maybe eleven o'clock we'd be dozing off. Our teachers would send notes to the house telling Mom that we were inattentive. The only thing I'd make fairly good grades on was spelling. I couldn't do anything else. Many times we never did our homework, because we were out in the fields. The teachers couldn't understand that. I would get whacked there also.

I would carry boxes for Mom to pack the carrots in. I would pull the carrots out and she would sort them into different sizes. I would get water for her to drink. When you're picking tomatoes, the boxes are heavy. They weigh about thirty pounds. They're dropped very hard on the trucks so they have to be sturdy.

The hardest would be thinning and hoeing with a short handled hoe.

The fields would be about a half mile long. You would be bending & stooping all day.

Some times you would have hard ground & by the time you got home, your hands would be full of calluses.

You'd have a backache

I remember when we just got into California from Arizona to pick up the carrot harvest. It was very cold & very windy out in the fields. We just had a little old blanket for the four of us kids in the tent. We were freezin' our tail off.

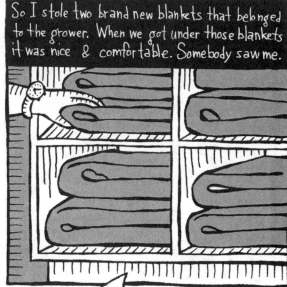

So I stole two brand new blankets that belonged to the grower. When we got under those blankets it was nice & comfortable. Somebody saw me.

The next day the grower told my Mom he'd turn us in unless we gave him back his blankets sterilized. So my Mom & I & my kid brother went to the river & cut some wood & made a fire & boiled the water & she scrubbed the blankets.

CRACK!

She hung them out to dry, ironed them & sent them back to the grower. We got a spanking for that.

I remember this labor camp that was run by the city. It was a POW camp for German soldiers. They put families in there & it would have barbed wire all around it. If you were out after ten o'clock at night, you couldn't get back until the next day at four in the morning.

NO TRESPASSING

GATES CLOSE AT 10:00 PM

We didn't know the rules. Nobody told us. We went to visit some relatives. We got back at ten thirty & they wouldn't let us in. So we slept in the pickup outside the gate, In the morning they let us in, we had a fast breakfast and went to work in the fields.

FEUD

ÑA

El Patrón (the boss)

TORR

The grower would keep the families apart, hoping they'd fight against each other. He'd have three or four camps and he'd have people over here pitted against people over there. For jobs, he'd give the best crops to the people he thought were the fastest workers. This way he kept us going harder & harder, competing.

When I was sixteen, I had my first taste as foreman. Handling braceros, aliens, that came from México to work. They'd bring these people to work over here and then send them back to México after the season was over. My job was to make sure they did a good job and pushin' 'em even harder. I was a company man, yes.

My parents needed money & I wanted to make sure they were proud of me. A foreman is recognized. I was very naive. Even though I was pushing the workers, I knew their problems.

ALIEN LABORER'S PERMIT

Flores Magón, José

Morelos, MX

May 05, 1920

MEXICO

3126975

José Flores M.

¿Que quieres escribir primo?

They didn't know how to write, so I would write letters home for them.

I would take 'em to town, buy their clothes, outside of the company stores.

Woolworth

OPEN

He had paid me $1.10 an hour. The farm workers pay was raised to 82.5¢. But even the braceros were making more money than me, because they were working piecework. I asked for more money. The manager said, "If you don't like it you can quit." I quit and joined the Marine Corps.

I joined the Marine Corps at seventeen. I was very mixed up.

I wanted to be a first-class citizen. I wanted to be accepted & I was very proud of my uniform. My Mom didn't want to sign the papers, but she knew I had to better myself & maybe I'd get an education in the services. I did many jobs. I took a civil service exam & was very proud when I passed. Most of the others were college kids. There were only three Chicanos in the group of sixty. I got a job as a correctional officer in the state prison. I quit after eight months because I couldn't take the misery I saw. They wanted me to use a rubber hose on some of the prisoners—mostly Chicanos & blacks. I couldn't do it. They called me chicken livered because I didn't want to hit nobody. They constantly harassed me after that. I didn't quit because I was afraid of them, but because they were trying to make me into a mean man. This was Soledad State Prison.

CUTS OF BEEF

chuck | prime rib | porter house | sirloin | rump

brisket | plate | flank | round

CUTS OF WORKER

grapes

carrots | strawberries | asparagus | tomatoes

celery | broccoli

CROPS = BIG $

melons | avocado

lettuce

I began to see how everything was so wrong. When growers can have an intricate watering system to irrigate their crops but can't have running water inside the houses of the workers. Veterinarians tend to the needs of domestic animals, but they can't have medical care for the workers. They can have subsidies for the growers but they can't have adequate unemployment compensation for the workers. They treat him like a farm implement. In fact they treat their implements better and their domestic animals better. They have heat and insulated barns for the animals but the workers live in beat up shacks with no heat at all.

Illness in the fields is 120% higer than the average rate for the industry.

It's mostly back trouble, rheumatism, & arthritis, because of the damp weather & cold. Stoop labor is hard on a person. TB is high. & now b/c of pesticides we have many respiratory diseases.

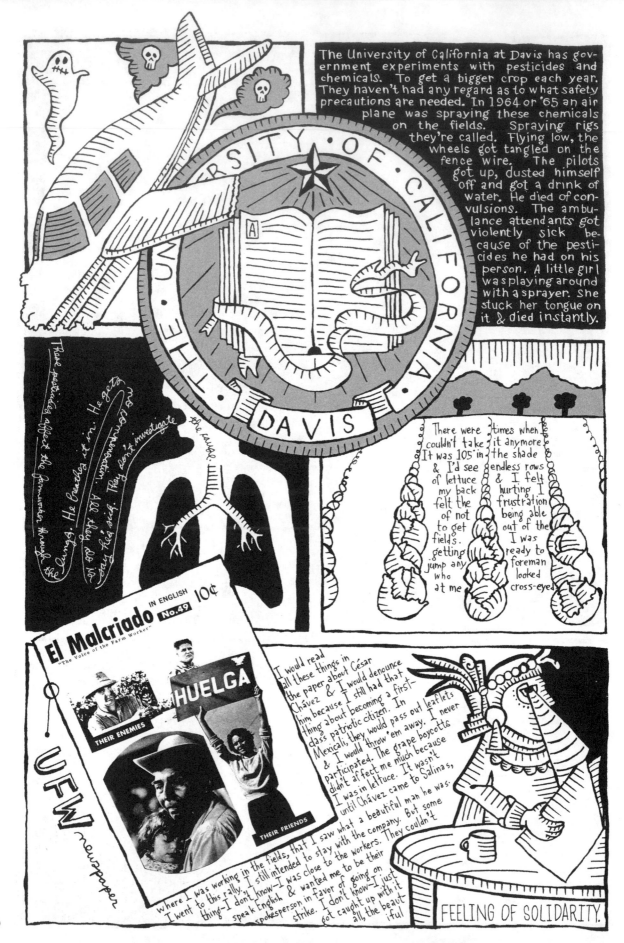

The University of California at Davis has government experiments with pesticides and chemicals. To get a bigger crop each year. They haven't had any regard as to what safety precautions are needed. In 1964 or '65 an airplane was spraying these chemicals on the fields. Spraying rigs they're called. Flying low, the wheels got tangled on the fence wire. The pilots got up, dusted himself off and got a drink of water. He died of convulsions. The ambulance attendants got violently sick because of the pesticides he had on his person. A little girl was playing around with a sprayer. She stuck her tongue on it & died instantly.

THE UNIVERSITY · OF · CALIFORNIA

A

DAVIS

These pesticides affect the farmworker through the lungs. He breathes it in. He gets no compensation. All they do is spray his suit. They don't investigate the cause.

There were times when I couldn't take it anymore. It was 105° in the shade & I'd see endless rows of lettuce & I felt my back hurting I felt the frustration of not being able to get out of the fields. I was getting ready to jump any foreman who looked at me cross-eyed

El Malcriado IN ENGLISH 10¢
"The Voice of the Farm Worker" No.49

HUELGA

THEIR ENEMIES

THEIR FRIENDS

UFW newspaper

I would read all these things in the paper about César Chávez & I would denounce him because I still had that thing about becoming a first-class patriotic citizen. In Mexicali, they would pass out leaflets & I would throw 'em away. I never participated. The grape boycotts didn't affect me much because I was in lettuce. It wasn't until Chávez came to Salinas, where I was working in the fields, that I saw what a beautiful man he was. I went to this rally. I still intended to stay with the company. But some thing—I don't know—I was close to the workers. They couldn't speak English & wanted me to be their spokesperson in favor of going on strike. I don't know—I just got caught up with it all, the beautiful

FEELING OF SOLIDARITY.

20

You'd see people on picket lines at four in the morning, at the camp fires, heating up beans and tortillas. It gave me a sense of belonging. These were my own people and they wanted change. I knew this is what I was looking for. I just didn't know it before. My mom had always wanted me to better myself. I wanted to better myself because of her. Now when the strike started, I told her I was going to join the union and the whole movement. I told her I was going to work without pay. She said she was proud of me. (His eyes glisten, a long, long pause) See I told her I wanted to be with my people. If I were a company man, nobody would like me anymore. I had to belong to somebody and this was it right here. She said, "I pushed you in your early years to try to better yourself and get a social position. But I see that's not the answer."

All kinds of people are farm workers, not just Chicanos. We have Puerto Ricans and Appalachians too, Arabs, some Japanese, some Chinese. At one time they used us against each other. But now they can't & they're scared, the growers. They can organize conglomerates, yet when we try organization to better our lives, they are afraid. Suffering people never dreamed it could be different. César Chávez tells them this & they grasp the idea — and this is what scares the growers.

Now the machines are coming in. It takes skill to operate them. But anybody can be taught. We feel that migrant workers should be given the chance. They got one for grapes. They got one for lettuce. They have cotton machines that took jobs away from thousands of farm workers.

If people could see—in the winter ice on the fields. We'd be on our knees all day long. We'd build fires & warm up real fast and go back onto the ice.

INVIERNO

We'd be picking watermelons in 105 degrees all day long.

VERANO

These dilapidated structures are supplied by the growers.

CAMPO

If I had enough money, I would take busloads of people out to the fields and into the labor camps. Then they'd know how that fine salad got on their table.

...on your left, ladies and gentlemen, you see lettuce fields stretching toward the horizon.

Pecking Order

27

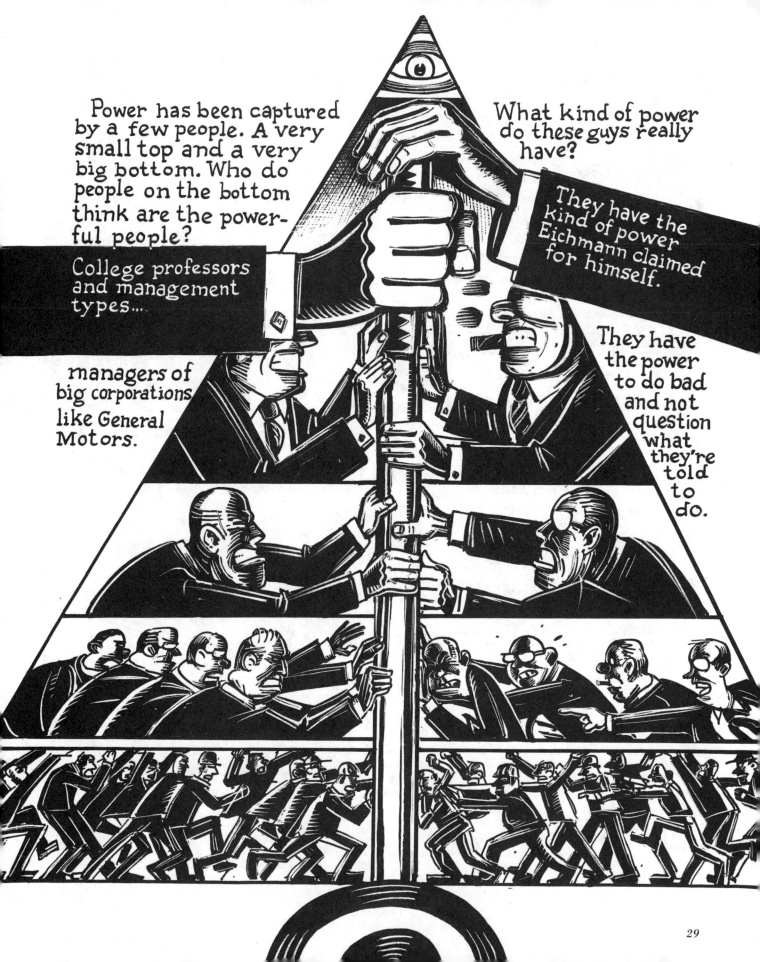

I came into consciousness during the fifties, when Joe McCarthy was running around...

Like many people my age—I'm now thirty-seven—I was aware something was terribly wrong.

I floundered around for two years in college, was disappointed, and enlisted in the army...

I was NCO* for my company. During a discussion I said if I was a black guy, I would refuse to serve...

I ended up being sent to division headquarters and locked up for two years so I wouldn't be able to talk to anybody, HA!

At San Francisco State, I got involved with the farm workers movement. I'd give speeches on a box in front of the Commons...

Then I'd go out and fight jocks behind the gym for an hour and a half. HAH!

In '64 I resigned as student body president and went to Mississippi to work for SNCC* I spent three years working in the black communities in San Francisco...

At that point... WELCOME TO KENTUCKY

I figured it was time to work with whites...

* Noncommissioned officer
* Student Nonviolent Coordinating Committee

30

My father was from South Carolina. I learned you had to build a base with white people on the fringe of the South. Hopefully you'd build an alliance between blacks and whites...

I came to East Kentucky and put together a fairly solid organization of Appalachian people in Pike County...

It's a single industry area, coal. You either work for the coal company or you don't work. Sixty percent of its people live on incomes lower than the government's guidelines for rural areas.

They dug down in their pockets and they'd take care of me like I was a cousin. But they didn't see me as one of them.

I'm not a coal miner...

I'm an organizer.

If they're going to save themselves, they're going to have to do it themselves. I have some skills that can help them.

I did this job for three years.

MINE 328

C & D

EIGHT HOURS
UNITED
OF
AMERICA
MINE WORKERS

The word organizer has been romanticized You get the vision of a mystical being doing mystical things...

ORGANIZER

Most people were raised to think they are not worthy...

An organizer is a guy who brings in new members. I don't feel I've had a good day unless I've talked with at least one new person.

We have a meeting and I sit next to the new guy, so everybody has to take the new guy as an equal. You do that a couple of times and the guy's got strength enough to be part of the group. You must listen to them and tell them again and again they are important, that they have the stuff to do the job. They don't have to shuck themselves about not being good enough, not worthy.

School is a process of taking beautiful kids who are filled with life and beating them into happy slavery.

That's as true of an executive as it is for the poor.

You don't find allies on the basis of the brotherhood of man. People are tied into their immediate problems.

They have a difficult time worrying about other people's. Our society is so structured that everybody is supposed to be selfish as hell and screw the other guy. Christian brotherhood is enlightened self-interest.

Most sins committed on poor people are by people who've come to help them.

I came to Pike County as a stranger, but I came with credentials, so what I'm saying is verifiable. It's possible to take on an outfit like Bethlehem Steel and lick 'em.

Nobody believed PCCA* could stop Bethlehem from strip mining. What they wanted was a park. Bethlehem said, "Go to hell, you're just a bunch of crummy Appalachians." If I could get that park for them, they would believe it's possible to do other things...

Most people in their guts don't believe it. Gee it's great when all of a sudden they realize it's possible. They become alive!

So I got together twenty or thirty people I saw as leaders. I said, "let's get that park." They said "we can't." I said, "We can. If we let all the big wheels around the country know and everybody starts calling, writing and hounding Bethlehem they have to give us the park."

That's exactly what happened.

Bethlehem thought; This is getting to be a pain in the ass. We'll give them the park and they'll shut up on strip mining. We haven't shut up on strip mining, but we got the park!

Four thousand people from Pike County drove up and watched those bulldozers grading down that park. It was an incredible victory...

*Pike County Citizens Association

34

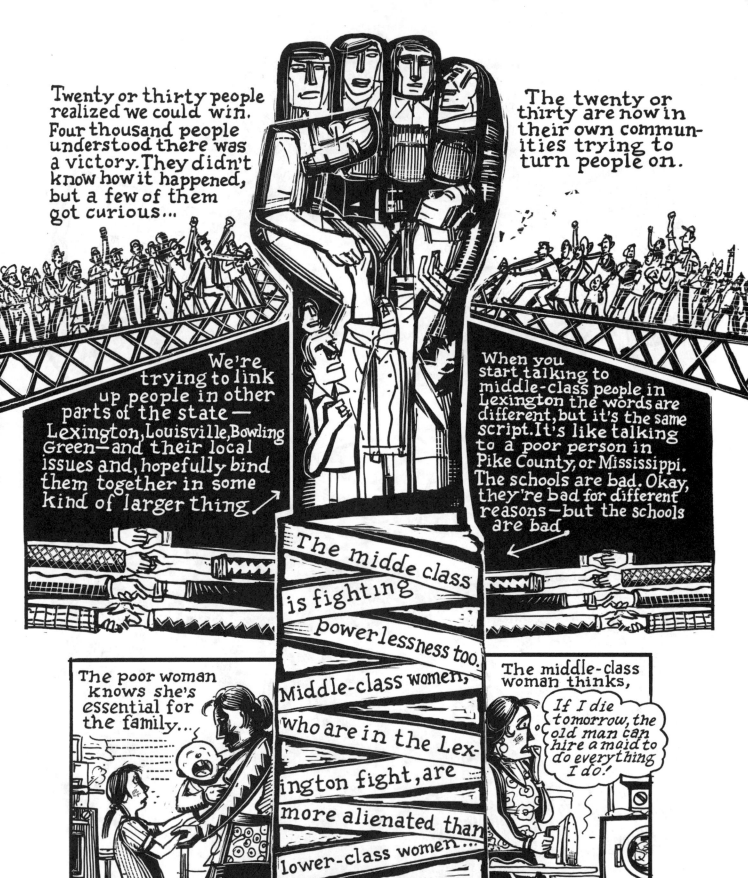

Twenty or thirty people realized we could win. Four thousand people understood there was a victory. They didn't know how it happened, but a few of them got curious...

The twenty or thirty are now in their own communities trying to turn people on.

We're trying to link up people in other parts of the state— Lexington, Louisville, Bowling Green—and their local issues and, hopefully bind them together in some kind of larger thing

When you start talking to middle-class people in Lexington the words are different, but it's the same script. It's like talking to a poor person in Pike County, or Mississippi. The schools are bad. Okay, they're bad for different reasons—but the schools are bad

The middle class is fighting powerlessness too. Middle-class women, who are in the Lexington fight, are more alienated than lower-class women...

The poor woman knows she's essential for the family...

The middle-class woman thinks,

If I die tomorrow, the old man can hire a maid to do everything I do!

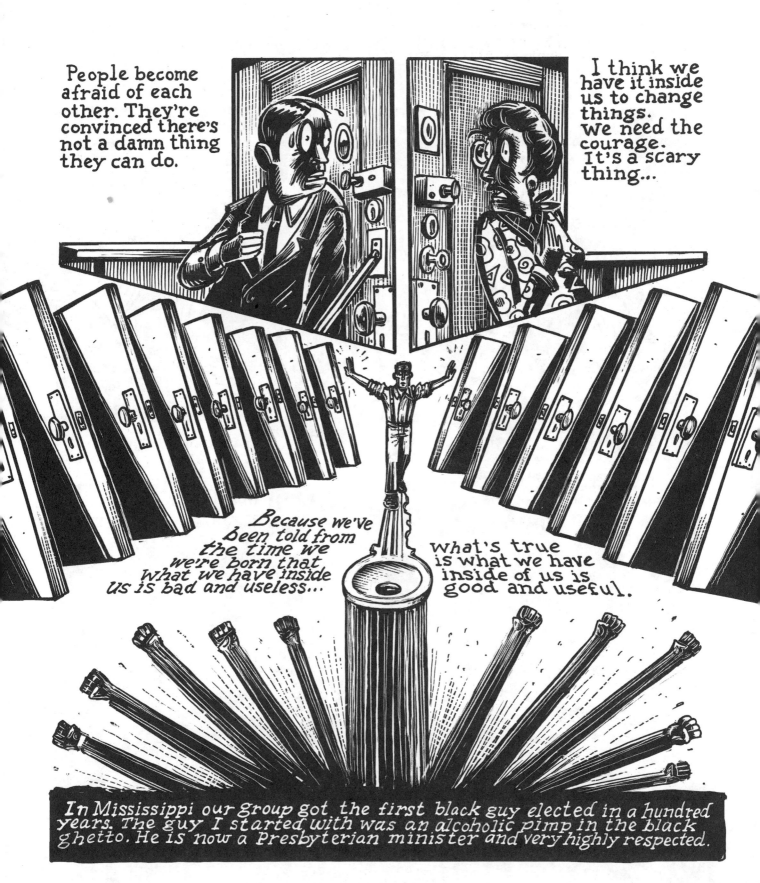

People become afraid of each other. They're convinced there's not a damn thing they can do.

I think we have it inside us to change things. We need the courage. It's a scary thing...

Because we've been told from the time we we're born that what we have inside us is bad and useless... what's true is what we have inside of us is good and useful.

In Mississippi our group got the first black guy elected in a hundred years. The guy I started with was an alcoholic pimp in the black ghetto. He is now a Presbyterian minister and very highly respected.

Hooker

As told to Studs Terkel by Roberta Victor Excerpted and illustrated by SABRINA JONES

I was about fifteen.

I was sitting in a coffee shop in the Village, and a friend of mine came by.

I've got a cab waiting. Hurry up. You can make $50 in 20 minutes.

Looking back, I wonder why I was so willing to run out and turn a trick.

I learned it from the society around me, just as a woman.

Don't sell yourself cheap.

Is it proper to kiss on the first date?

It may not be, but...

dinner on the second date, it's proper...

a bottle of perfume on the third date, let him touch you above the waist.

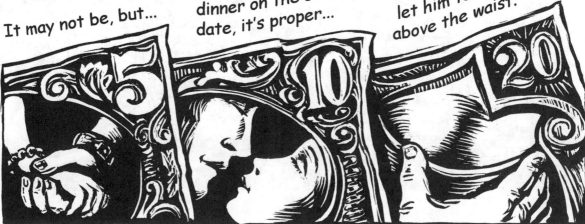

We took a cab to midtown Manhattan, we went to a penthouse.

731

He wanted to watch two women make love, then... have sex with me. It was barely sex.

He barely touched me and we were finished.

Of course we faked it, the woman and me. You always fake it. He's paying for something he didn't really get. That's the only way you can keep any self-respect.

You were the lowest of the low if you allowed yourself to feel anything with a trick.

I came downtown.

I'm the same as I was 20 minutes ago, except that now I have $50 in my pocket.*

I let my friend know I was available for more.

*At time, many people worked for eighty dollars a week.

Books of phone numbers were passed around from call girl to call girl.

Numbers of folks who are quite respectable, not liable to pull a knife or cheat you out of money. There's three or four groups:

the wealthy executive, the social figure, the quiet, independently wealthy type, the entertainer, the crowd that runs around the night spots.

We used to share numbers.

Call so-and-so, that's a $50 trick.

They give you $25. Then the number was theirs.

It doesn't get conducted as a business transaction. The myth is that it's a social occasion.

I'm a friend of so-and-so's and she thought it would be nice if we got together.

Why don't you come over for a drink?

You have to look as if you belong in those buildings on Park Avenue.

You're expected not to look cheap,

not to look hard.

Youth is the premium.

At the beginning I was very excited.

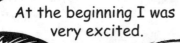

But in order to continue I had to turn myself off.

I found I couldn't turn myself back on.

I was numb - emotionally, sexually numb.

At first I felt like I was putting one over on all the poor slobs who go to work at 8:30 and come home at 5.

I spent my mornings doing my nails.

...going to the beauty parlor, going shopping...

It was usually two tricks a night.

I didn't know what the inside of a subway smelled like. I ate in all the best restaurants and drank in all the best clubs.

Almost all the call girls I knew were involved in drugs.

You wake up at noon. There's not very much to do until 9 or 10 that night. Everybody else is at work, so you shoot heroin.

After a while, the work became a means of supplying drugs...

...instead of the drugs being something we took when we were bored.

The doormen smirk. The cabdriver knows exactly where you're going,

riding up Park Avenue at 10 o'clock at night, for Christ sake.

You leave there and go back - to what? Really, to what? To an emptiness.

When I was a call girl I looked down on streetwalkers.

I had to work an awful lot harder for the same money when I was a streetwalker. I remember

being raped, having my money stolen, having to jump out of a second story window.

What led you to the streets?

My drug habit. It got larger. I started looking bad.

As a call girl, you must look presentable, not like death on a soda cracker.

When I hit the streets, I tried to stick to at least...

20 dollars.

...folks would laugh.

I needed $100 a night. It meant seven or eight tricks a night. I was out on the street from 9 o'clock at night till 4 in the morning.

For the first time, I ran the risk of being busted. The law says to arrest a woman for prostitution, she has to mention money and she has to tell you what she'll do for it.

It's a nice night isn't it?

Are you busy?

Yes.

Not particularly.

I have 15 dollars and I'm very lonely.

Then you spell out exactly what you're willing to do.

I was trapped by cops several times. I remember passing a banana truck.

It didn't dawn on me that it was strange to be selling bananas at 3 o'clock in the morning.

The banana salesman was a vice squad cop.

I got 3 years for that one.

Once I got really trapped. The cop isn't supposed to undress. If you can describe the color of his shorts, it's an invalid arrest.

Not only did he show me his shorts, he went to bed with me. Then he pulled a badge and a gun and he busted me.

What's the status of the streetwalker in prison?

It's fine. Everybody there had been hustling. It's status in reverse. Anybody saying they could never hustle is looked down upon as being somewhat crazy.

For a couple years I worked in a Mexican version of a French whorehouse. The men would come and we'd parade in front of them.

The Mexicans wanted American girls. The Americans wanted Mexican girls.

I was in great demand. I was the only American.

That was really hard work. American tricks come as quickly as they can.

Mexicans would hold back and make me work for my money.

The junk down there was quite cheap and quite good.

My habit was quite large.

I loved dope more than anything else around.

After a while I couldn't differentiate between working and not working. All men were tricks, all relationships were acting. I was completely turned off.

You become your job. I became what I did.

Even when I wasn't hustling, I was a hustler.

I became cold. I became hard. I became turned off. I became numb.

I don't think it's terribly different from someone who works on the assembly line 40 hours a week and comes home numb, dehumanized.

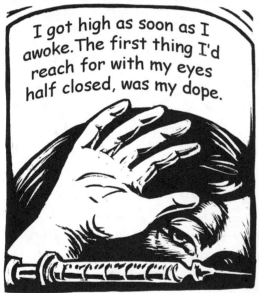

I got high as soon as I awoke. The first thing I'd reach for with my eyes half closed, was my dope.

I didn't like my work. It was messy. Here's all these guys slobbering over you all night long. What enabled me to do it was being high, high and numb.

The overt hustling society is a microcosm of the rest of society.

As a cold manipulative hustler, I had a lot.

As a bright, assertive woman, I had no power.

All I did was act out the reality of American womanhood.

Barbara Terwilliger ~ illustrated by Joan Reilly

SHE IS IN HER THIRTIES. SHE HAS AN INDEPENDENT INCOME AND IS COMFORTABLY OFF.

IT CAN BE SPLENDID NOT TO WORK FOR A WHILE, BECAUSE IT CHANGES THE RHYTHM — YOU CAN REFLECT ON WHAT YOU'VE DONE. THERE'S NO FEELING OF BEING INDOLENT.

DURING HER LESS AFFLUENT DAYS, SHE HAD WORKED AS AN ACTRESS, AS A SALESWOMAN, ENGAGED IN MARKET RESEARCH, AND HAD OTHER ASSORTED OCCUPATIONS.

I LIKE BEING BY MYSELF FOR LONG PERIODS OF TIME AND DO NOT NEED AN OCCUPATION.

AFTER TWO MONTHS THOUGH, IT DOESN'T WORK FOR ME. I BEGIN TO FEEL THE NEED FOR A RAISON D'ETRE.

FWEEEEE

UNLESS I'M IN LOVE. IF I SHOULD BE IN LOVE, AFTER MONTHS I WOULD BEGIN TO FEEL PARASITIC AND INDOLENT.

EEEE

WHAT'S LOVE GOT TO DO WITH IT?

OH, WELL, LOVE IS A WOMAN'S OCCUPATION. HAHA!! IT'S A FULL-TIME OCCUPATION IF YOU'RE MARRIED.

SINCE I'M NOT MARRIED, I'M TALKING ABOUT A LOVE AFFAIR. IF YOU HAVE ANY KIND OF EGO, YOU CAN'T MAKE A LOVE AFFAIR A JUSTIFICATION FOR LIFE.

51

I TRIED TO PAY VERY MUCH ATTENTION TO THE WORDS I WAS TYPING DOWN. I CARE ABOUT LANGUAGE. SOME OF THE WORDS WERE REPUGNANT TO ME. IF I WERE HAVING TO TYPE SOME PORNO STUFF OR HAVING TO SAY,...

"Dry cereal is the best thing to feed one's kids night and day,

they're going to flourish eating Crunchy Puffs"

...I WOULDN'T BE ABLE TO DO IT.

BUT THE PROCESS GAVE ME SATISFACTION. THERE WEREN'T VERY MANY ERASURES. IT WAS NEAT.

I REALLY FEEL WORK IS GORGEOUS. IT'S THE ONLY THING YOU CAN DEPEND ON IN LIFE. YOU CAN'T DEPEND ON LOVE. OH, LOVE IS QUITE EPHEMERAL.

PRRRRRRRR...

WORK HAS A DIGNITY YOU CAN COUNT ON.

WORK HAS TO BE A GAME IN ORDER FOR IT TO BE WELL-DONE.

YOU HAVE TO BE ABLE TO PLAY IN IT, TO COMPETE WITH YOURSELF.

YOU PUSH YOURSELF TO YOUR LIMITS IN ORDER TO ENJOY IT.

THERE'S QUITE A WONDERFUL RHYTHM YOU CAN FIND YOURSELF INVOLVED IN, IN THE PROCESS OF ANY KIND OF WORK. IT CAN BE WAXING A FLOOR OR WASHING DISHES.

I WORKED FOR AN EMPLOYMENT AGENCY, DOING PLACEMENTS. THEY DIVIDED THE GIRLS INTO PLACEABLES AND UNPLACEABLES. I WAS USUALLY DRAWN TO THE UNPLACEABLES.

THESE WERE GIRLS WHO SEEMED TO ME TO HAVE SOME SORT OF— MAYBE INCHOATE — CREATIVE GIFTS. THEY WANTED JOBS WHERE THEY COULD FEEL AS INDIVIDUALS.

THE GIRLS WHOSE HAIR WAS NOT IN PLACE, WHO LOOKED UNTIDY, WHO WEREN'T GOING TO BE THAT EASILY ACCEPTED. THERE WERE SOME ECCENTRICITIES INVOLVED.

I WOULD SPEND MOST OF MY TIME WITH THEM. I WOULD MAKE PHONE CALLS TO — GOD FORGIVE — ADVERTISING AGENCIES, RADIO STATIONS.

HELLO, WBZR?

IF YOU CONCENTRATED ON THE PLACEABLES, YOU MADE MONEY. THESE WERE THE GIRLS WHO CAME OFF THE PRODUCTION LINE OF HIGH SCHOOLS, PARTICULARLY THE CATHOLIC SCHOOLS.

FIRST NATIONAL? THIS IS BARBARA TERWILLIGER...

THEY SEEMED TO BE TRACTABLE YOUNG GIRLS. THEY WENT INTO BANKS AS FILING CLERKS IN THOSE DAYS. YOU CALLED THE BANKS AND YOU HAD YOUR CARD FILE AND YOU SENT THE GIRL OVER TO THE JOB.

YOU COULD BE A MASS PRODUCTION WORKER YOURSELF, WORKING THESE GIRLS INTO THE SYSTEM. THERE WERE NO TOUGH CORNERS, NOTHING ABRASIVE. ONE OF MY COLLEAGUES MADE TWO HUNDRED DOLLARS A WEEK SHOVELING PEOPLE INTO THESE SLOTS.

I WASN'T DOING WHAT THE OTHER GIRLS AT THE DESKS WERE DOING. I FOUND MYSELF HAUNTED AT NIGHT BY THE UNPLACEABLE GIRLS. THE UNPLACEABLE GIRLS WERE ME. IF I FAILED THEM, I WAS FAILING MYSELF.

I COULDN'T MAKE ANY MONEY. I QUIT IN THREE WEEKS. THEY PROBABLY WOULD HAVE FIRED ME ANYWAY.

TIP=TOP
Employment Agency

THEY WERE PRETTY INTENSE WEEKS. I SUFFERED A LOT. I NEEDED THE MONEY. I WAS LIVING ON PRACTICALLY NOTHING. MY GIRLS WERE LOSERS. I FOUND IT UNBEARABLE TO REJECT THEM.

YOU SAY, "WE HAVE NOTHING FOR YOU," AND SEND THEM AWAY. YOUR TIME IS MONEY, YOU WORK ON COMMISSION. THERE WAS A CODE ON THE APPLICATION BLANK, SO YOU COULD GIVE THE GIRL THE BRUSH-OFF AND SHE'D NEVER KNOW WHY.

THERE WERE A COUPLE OF TIMES I FOUND JOBS FOR THE UNKEMPT GIRLS, WHOSE STOCKINGS WERE BAGGY. AND THERE WAS EVEN SOME PLEASURE IN PLACING THOSE SWEET, NAIVE GIRLS, WHO WANTED NOTHING BETTER THAN TO WORK IN BANKS AND THEY WERE GRATEFUL.

EVEN THERE, THE PROCESS — BEING PART OF SOMETHING, MAKING SOMETHING HAPPEN, WAS IMPORTANT. THAT'S THE DIFFERENCE BETWEEN BEING ALIVE AND BEING DEAD.

NOW I'M NOT MAKING ANYTHING HAPPEN.

EVERYONE NEEDS TO FEEL THEY HAVE A PLACE IN THE WORLD. IT WOULD BE UNBEARABLE NOT TO. I DON'T LIKE TO FEEL SUPERFLUOUS. ONE NEEDS TO BE NEEDED.

MROW!

I'M SAYING BEING IDLE AND LEISURED, DOING NOTHING, IS TRAGIC AND DISGRACEFUL. EVERYONE MUST HAVE AN OCCUPATION.

YAWN

WHAT WILL I DO TODAY?

LOVE DOESN'T SUFFICE. IT DOESN'T FILL UP ENOUGH HOURS. I DON'T MEAN WORK MUST BE ACTIVITY FOR ACTIVITY'S SAKE. I DON'T MEAN OBSESSIVE, EMPTY MOVING AROUND. I MEAN CREATING SOMETHING NEW.

BUT IDLENESS IS AN EVIL. I DON'T THINK MAN CAN MAINTAIN HIS BALANCE OR SANITY IN IDLENESS.

HUMAN BEINGS MUST WORK TO CREATE SOME COHERENCE. YOU DO IT ONLY THROUGH WORK AND THROUGH LOVE, AND YOU CAN ONLY COUNT ON WORK.

Footwork

Jack Spiegel, SHOE WORKERS UNION ORGANIZER

ABOUT SIXTY PER CENT IN THE INDUSTRY ARE WOMEN. IN SOME SHOPS, IT GOES AS HIGH AS SEVENTY PER CENT. A GREAT MANY ARE SPANISH-SPEAKING AND BLACKS. IT'S LOW PAYING WORK. THE AVERAGE WAGE IN THE SHOE INDUSTRY TODAY IS A LITTLE OVER A HUNDRED DOLLARS A WEEK. THERE ARE ALL KINDS OF WORK STOPPAGES. EVEN CONSERVATIVE WORKERS ARE MILITANT IN THE SHOPS.

WUDDYA MEAN I'M GOOFIN' AROUND?

TRADITIONALLY, THE SHOE INDUSTRY HAS BEEN ON PIECEWORK. WE DISCOURAGE IT AND IN MANY CASES STRUGGLE WITH OUR OWN PEOPLE. THEY CAN PICK UP TWENTY-FIVE, THIRTY PER CENT OVER THEIR TIME WEEK. BUT WE DON'T ACCEPT THE PHILOSOPHY THAT YOU'VE GOT TO WORK 'TIL YOU DROP. SMALL SHOPS ARE GOING OUT OF BUSINESS BECAUSE THEY CAN'T COMPETE WITH THE GIANTS. THERE'S BEEN A LOT OF MERGERS IN THE SHOE INDUSTRY. IMPORTATION HAS CUT INTO A THIRD OF THE SHOES BEING SOLD IN OUR COUNTRY. SHOES ARE BROUGHT IN FROM SPAIN, JAPAN, ITALY. THE AVERAGE WAGE IN THIS COUNTRY IS $2.00 ～ IN ITALY IT IS $1.10.

HOW CAN WE COMPETE WITH THESE PEOPLE OVERSEAS? THEY GOT LOWER STANDARDS OF LIVING!

THE SAME MANUFACTURERS WHO EXPLOIT HERE, OPEN UP FACTORIES THERE, BRING THE SHOES HERE, FINISH 'EM IN SOME PLACES AND PUT A "MADE IN AMERICA" LABEL ON THEM. THE CONSUMER THINKS HE'S GETTING A BREAK. THEY GET IT A LITTLE CHEAPER, BUT THE QUALITY AND WORKMANSHIP MAY NOT BE AS GOOD.

LATELY YOU'VE BEEN CARRYING SOME LOW COST SHOES. THEY'RE NOT HALF BAD.

UP TO ABOUT TWELVE YEARS AGO WE HAD ABOUT A QUARTER OF A MILLION WORKERS. THERE ARE NOW LESS THAN 170,000. IN THE NEXT 10-15 YEARS, IT MAY DIMINISH TO LESS THAN 50,000. WHAT HAPPENED TO WATCHMAKING MAY HAPPEN TO US. IT'S HAPPENED TO TEXTILES, TOO, WHERE HALF THE WORKERS LOST THEIR JOBS IN THE PAST 20 YEARS.

FOR RENT

CLOSED

UNITED COTTON INDUSTRIES

IF SOME MEASURES AREN'T TAKEN BY THE GOVERNMENT TO TAX THOSE WHO SEND MONEY OUT AND ESTABLISH THOSE FACTORIES IN OTHER COUNTRIES, AND TAKE JOBS AWAY FROM PEOPLE HERE, IT WILL BE GOOD-BYE TO THE AMERICAN SHOE INDUSTRY. THOSE IN THEIR 60's WILL RETIRE. THOSE THAT ARE STILL ABLE TO WORK WILL FIND IT MORE DIFFICULT.

EVERYTHING **LOOKS** FRESH AND NICE.
YOU'RE NOT AWARE THAT IN THE BACK-ROOM IT **STINKS** AND THERE'S CRATES ALL OVER THE PLACE AND THE WALLS ARE MESSED UP.
THERE'S GRAFFITI AND PEOPLE ARE SWEARING AND YELLING AT EACH OTHER.
YOU WALK THROUGH THE DOOR, THE MUSIC STARTS PLAYING, EVERYTHING IS PRETTY.

YOU TALK IN HUSHED TONES AND ARE VERY RESPECTFUL.

YOU WEAR A BADGE WITH YOUR NAME ON IT. I ONCE MET SOMEONE I KNEW YEARS AGO. I REMEMBERED HIS NAME.

WE TALKED ABOUT THIS AND THAT. AS HE LEFT HE SAID, "IT WAS NICE TALKING TO YOU BRETT." I FELT **GREAT**, HE REMEMBERED ME. THEN I LOOKED DOWN AT MY NAME-PLATE. **OH SHIT**. HE DIDN'T REMEMBER ME AT ALL, HE JUST READ THE NAME-PLATE. I WISH I PUT IRVING DOWN ON MY NAME-PLATE. IF HE'D HAVE SAID, "OH YES, IRVING, HOW COULD I FORGET YOU?" I'D HAVE BEEN READY FOR HIM. THERE'S NOTHING PERSONAL HERE.

YOU HAVE TO BE RESPECTFUL TO EVERYONE — THE CUSTOMERS, TO THE MANAGER, TO THE CHECKERS. THERE'S A SIGN ON THE CASH REGISTER THAT SAYS, "SMILE AT THE CUSTOMER, SAY HELLO TO THE CUSTOMER." IT'S ASSUMED IF YOU'RE A BOX-BOY YOU'RE REALLY THERE BECAUSE YOU WANT TO BE A MANAGER SOME DAY.
SO YOU LEARN ALL THE LITTLE THINGS YOU HAVE **ABSOLUTELY** NO INTEREST IN LEARNING

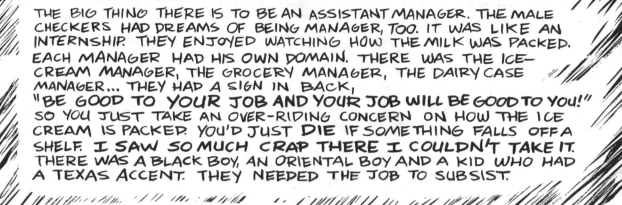

THE BIG THING THERE IS TO BE AN ASSISTANT MANAGER. THE MALE CHECKERS HAD DREAMS OF BEING MANAGER, TOO. IT WAS LIKE AN INTERNSHIP. THEY ENJOYED WATCHING HOW THE MILK WAS PACKED. EACH MANAGER HAD HIS OWN DOMAIN. THERE WAS THE ICE-CREAM MANAGER, THE GROCERY MANAGER, THE DAIRY CASE MANAGER... THEY HAD A SIGN IN BACK, "BE GOOD TO YOUR JOB AND YOUR JOB WILL BE GOOD TO YOU!" SO YOU JUST TAKE AN OVER-RIDING CONCERN ON HOW THE ICE CREAM IS PACKED. YOU'D JUST **DIE** IF SOMETHING FALLS OFF A SHELF. I SAW SO MUCH CRAP THERE I COULDN'T TAKE IT. THERE WAS A BLACK BOY, AN ORIENTAL BOY AND A KID WHO HAD A TEXAS ACCENT. THEY NEEDED THE JOB TO SUBSIST.

I GUESS I HAD THE LUXURY TO HATE IT AND QUIT.

GOOD RIDDANCE!

I'M NEVER COMING BACK!

WHEN I FIRST STARTED THERE, THE MANAGER SAID, "CUT YOUR HAIR, COME IN A WHITE SHIRT AND A TIE. BE HERE ON TIME!" YOU GET THERE AND HE ISN'T THERE. I JUST DIDN'T KNOW WHAT TO DO. THE CHECKER TURNS AROUND AND SAYS, "YOU NEW? WHAT'S YOUR NAME? BRETT? I'M PEGGY." AND THAT'S ALL THEY'LL SAY TO YOU AND THEY KEEP **THROWING** THINGS DOWN TO YOU.

DON'T PUT IT IN THAT— PUT IT IN THERE!

CRACKERS

BUT THEY WOULDN'T HELP YOU.

WHEN IT GOT SLOW, THE CHECKERS WOULD TALK ABOUT THE FUNNY THINGS THAT HAPPENED. ABOUT **US** AND **THEM.**
US BEING THE PEOPLE WHO WORKED THERE AND **THEM** BEING THE STUPID FOOLS WHO DIDN'T KNOW WHERE ANYTHING WAS—JUST CAME THROUGH AND MESSED EVERYTHING UP AND SHOPPED.
WE SERVE **THEM** BUT WE DON'T LIKE **THEM.**
WE KNOW WHAT TIME THE MARKET CLOSES, AND **THEY** DON'T. WE KNOW WHAT TO DO WITH THE COUPONS. THERE WAS A CAMARADERIE OF SORTS.

SHE ASKS ME WHERE IT WAS AND I SAID, "IN THE BACK." SO SHE GOES WALKING TO THE FRONT!

HEH, HEH.

SKRTCH SKRTCH

IT WASN'T HEALTHY THOUGH, IT WAS A PUT DOWN OF OTHERS.

THERE WAS ONE CHECKER WHO WAS ABSOLUTELY **VICIOUS**—

—HE TOOK GREAT DELIGHT IN MAKING EVERY LITTLE PROBLEM INTO A MAJOR CRISIS, FROM WHICH HE'D HAVE TO EMERGE VICTORIOUS.

YOU WERE **SUPPOSED** TO GIVE ME THIS COUPON AT THE **BEGINNING!**

OH, I'M SORRY.

NOW I GOTTA OPEN THE REGISTER AND GO THROUGH THE WHOLE THING **AGAIN.**

MADAM, I DON'T WATCH OUT FOR **EVERY** CUSTOMER. I CAN'T MANAGE YOUR LIFE!

A PUTDOWN.

YOU HAD TO KEEP YOUR APRON CLEAN. YOU COULDN'T LEAN BACK ON THE RAILINGS. YOU COULDN'T TALK TO THE CHECKERS.
YOU COULDN'T ACCEPT TIPS--
-- OKAY, I'M OUTSIDE AND I PUT IT IN THE CAR. FOR A LOT OF PEOPLE, THE NATURAL REACTION IS TO TAKE OUT A QUARTER AND GIVE IT TO ME.

I'D SAY, "I'M SORRY, I CAN'T." THEY'D GET OFFENDED. WHEN YOU GIVE SOMEONE A TIP, YOU'RE SORT OF *SUAVE*. YOU TAKE A QUARTER AND PUT IT IN THEIR PALM AND YOU EXPECT THEM TO SAY, "*OH, THANKS A LOT.*" WHEN YOU SAY, "I'M SORRY, I CAN'T." THEY FEEL A LITTLE PUT DOWN. THEY SAY, "NO ONE WILL KNOW." AND THEY PUT IT IN YOUR POCKET. YOU SAY, "I REALLY CAN'T."
IT GETS TO THE POINT WHERE YOU HAVE TO DO *PHYSICAL VIOLENCE* TO A PERSON TO AVOID BEING TIPPED. IT WAS NOT CONSISTENT WITH THE STORE'S PHILOSOPHY OF BEING CORDIAL. ACCEPTING TIPS WAS A CORDIAL THING AND MADE THE CUSTOMER FEEL GOOD. I JUST COULDN'T UNDERSTAND THE INCONGRUITY. ONE LADY ACTUALLY PUT IT IN MY SHIRT POCKET, GOT IN THE CAR AND DROVE AWAY. I WOULD HAVE HAD TO THROW THE QUARTER AT HER OR SOMETHING.

JIM'S THE BOSS. A FISH-TYPE HAND-
SHAKE. HE WAS BALDING AND IN HIS
MID-FORTIES.

A LOT OF MANAGERS ARE
THESE YOUNG, CLEAN-SHAVEN
NEATLY CROPPED PEOPLE IN
THEIR 20'S. SO JIM WOULD
SAY THINGS LIKE, "GROOVY."
YOU WERE SUPPOSED TO
GET A BREAK EVERY 2 HOURS.
I LIVED FOR THAT BREAK.
YOU'D GO OUTSIDE, TAKE
YOUR SHOES OFF AND BE
HUMAN AGAIN.

YOU HAD TO
REQUEST IT--

--AND WHEN
YOU TOOK IT-

WHY DO YOU
HAVE YOUR
SHOES OFF?

- THEY MADE
YOU FEEL GUILTY.

YOU GO UP AND
SAY, "JIM, CAN
I HAVE A
BREAK?" HE'D
SAY, "A BREAK,
YOU WANT A
BREAK, MAKE
IT A QUICK ONE,
9 AND ½ MIN-
UTES." ha-ha.
ONE TIME I
ASKED THE
ASSISTANT
MANAGER HENRY,
HE WAS OLDER
THAN JIM, "DO
YOU THINK I
CAN HAVE A
BREAK?"

YOU GOT A
BREAK WHEN
YOU WERE
HIRED!

ha-ha.

70

THE GUYS WHO LOAD THE SHELVES ARE A STEP ABOVE BOX-BOYS. IT WAS LIKE UPPER-CLASSMEN AT AN OFFICER CANDIDATE SCHOOL. THEY WOULD MAKE SURE YOU PRESCRIBED TO THE RULES, BECAUSE THEY WERE ONCE BOX-BOYS. THEY KNEW WHAT YOU'RE GOING THROUGH, YOUR ANXIETIES BUT INSTEAD OF MAKING IT EASIER FOR YOU, THEY'D MAKE IT HARDER,
IT'S LIKE
A MILITARY INSTITUTION.

HEY, WHY ARE YOU CARRYING THE BOX LIKE THAT? YOU'LL SPILL IT!

I KEPT GETTING BOX-BOYS WHO CAME UP TO ME—

HAS JIM TALKED TO YOU ABOUT YOUR HAIR?

HE'S GOING TO BECAUSE IT'S GETTING TOO LONG—

—YOU'D BETTER GET IT CUT OR GREASE IT OR SOMETHING.

—THEY TOOK DELIGHT IN IT.

THEY'D COME TO ME BEFORE JIM TOLD ME.

EVERYBODY WAS PUTTING EVERYBODY DOWN.

IT NEVER BOTHERED ME WHEN I PUT SOMETHING IN THE BAG WRONG. IN THE GENERAL SCHEME OF THINGS, IN THE LARGE QUESTIONS OF THE UNIVERSE, PUTTING A CAN OF DOG FOOD IN THE WRONG BAG IS NOT OF GREAT CONCERN.

THERE WERE A FEW CHECKERS THAT WERE NICE. THERE WAS ONE THAT WAS INCREDIBLY SAD. SHE COULD BE UNPLEASANT AT TIMES, BUT SHE WAS ONE OF THE FEW PEOPLE WHO GENUINELY WANTED TO TALK TO PEOPLE. SHE WAS SAYING HOW SHE WANTED TO GO TO SCHOOL AND TAKE COURSES SO SHE COULD GET SOME TEACHING CREDIT. SOMEONE ASKED HER, "WHY DON'T YOU?" SHE SAID, "I HAVE TO WORK HERE. MY HOURS ARE WRONG. I'D HAVE TO GET THEM CHANGED." THEY SAID, "WHY DON'T YOU?" SHE'D WORKED THERE FOR YEARS, SHE HAD SENIORITY. SHE SAID, "JIM WON'T LET ME." JIM WAS THE MANAGER. HE DIDN'T GIVE A DAMN. SHE WANTED TO GO BACK TO SCHOOL TO TEACH, BUT SHE CAN'T BECAUSE EVERYDAY SHE'S GOT TO GO TO THE SUPERMARKET AND LOAD GROCERIES. YET SHE WASN'T BITTER. IF SHE DIED A CHECKER AND NEVER ENRICHED HER LIFE, THAT WAS OK, BECAUSE THOSE WERE HER HOURS.

She has been a waitress in the same restaurant for twenty-three years. Many of its patrons are credit card carriers on an expense account. Her hours are from 5:00 P.M. to 2:00 A.M. six days a week. She arrives earlier "to get things ready... the silverware, the butter. When people come in and ask for you, you would like to be in a position to handle them all, because that means more money for you."

"I became a waitress because I needed money fast. My husband and I broke up and he left me with debts and three children. My baby was six months. The fast buck, your tips. The first ten dollar bill that I got as a tip, a Viking guy gave me. He was a very robust, terrific atheist. Made very good conversation for us, 'cause I am too."

Dolores Dante, Waitress

Today's Specials

Red Snapper
Grilled Tuna
Seafood Gumbo
over rice

Dolores

"Everyone says all waitresses have broken homes. What they don't realize is when people have broken homes they need to make money fast, and do this work. They don't have broken homes because they're waitresses."

adapted by **Lance Tooks**

74

I'M CALLED BY MY FIRST NAME. I LIKE MY NAME. I HATE TO BE CALLED MISS. EVEN WHEN I SERVE A LADY, A STRANGE WOMAN, I WILL NOT SAY MADAM. I HATE MA'AM. I ALWAYS SAY MILADY. IN THE AMERICAN LANGUAGE THERE IS NO WORD TO ADDRESS A WOMAN, TO INDICATE WHETHER SHE'S MARRIED OR UNMARRIED. SO I SAY MILADY. AND SOMETIMES I PLAYFULLY SAY TO THE MAN MILORD.

IT WOULD BE VERY TIRING IF I HAD TO SAY, "WOULD YOU LIKE A COCKTAIL?" AND SAY THAT OVER AND OVER. SO I COME OUT DIFFERENT FOR MY OWN ENJOYMENT. I WOULD SAY, "WHAT'S EXCITING AT THE BAR THAT I CAN OFFER?" MAYBE I'LL SAY, "ARE YOU IN THE MOOD FOR COFFEE?"

OR, "THE COFFEE SOUNDS EXCITING." JUST REPHRASE IT ENOUGH TO MAKE IT INTERESTING FOR ME. THAT WOULD MAKE THEM TAKE AN INTEREST. IT BECOMES THEATRICAL AND I FEEL LIKE *MATA HARI* AND IT INTOXICATES ME.

Dolores

PEOPLE IMAGINE A WAITRESS COULDN'T POSSIBLY THINK OR HAVE ANY KIND OF ASPIRATION OTHER THAN TO SERVE FOOD. WHEN SOMEBODY SAYS TO ME, "YOU'RE GREAT, HOW COME YOU'RE JUST A WAITRESS?"

JUST A WAITRESS. I'D SAY, "WHY, DON'T YOU THINK YOU DESERVE TO BE SERVED BY ME?" IT'S IMPLYING THAT *HE'S* NOT WORTHY, NOT THAT I'M NOT WORTHY. IT MAKES ME IRATE. I DON'T FEEL LOWLY AT ALL. I MYSELF FEEL SURE. I DON'T WANT TO CHANGE THE JOB. I LOVE IT.

TIPS? I FEEL LIKE *CARMEN.* IT'S LIKE A GYPSY HOLDING OUT A TAMBOURINE AND THEY THROW THE COIN. (LAUGHS.)

IF YOU LIKE PEOPLE, YOU'RE NOT THINKING OF THE TIPS. I NEVER COUNT MY MONEY AT NIGHT. I ALWAYS WAIT TILL MORNING. IF I THOUGHT ABOUT MY TIPS I'D BE UPTIGHT. I NEVER LOOK AT A TIP. YOU PICK IT UP FAST. I WOULD DO MY BOOKKEEPING IN THE MORNING. IT WOULD BE VERY DULL FOR ME TO KNOW I WAS MAKING SO MUCH AND NO MORE. I DO LIKE CHALLENGE.

AND IT ISN'T DEMEANING, NOT FOR ME.

THERE MIGHT BE OCCASIONS WHEN THE CUSTOMERS MIGHT INTEND TO MAKE IT DEMEANING— THE MAN ABOUT TOWN, THE CONVENTIONEER. WHEN THE TIME COMES TO PAY THE CHECK, HE WOULD DO LITTLE THINGS, "HOW MUCH SHOULD I GIVE YOU?" HE MIGHT MAKE AN ISSUE ABOUT IT.

I DID SAY TO ONE, "DON'T PLAY GOD WITH ME. DO WHAT YOU WANT."

THEN IT REALLY DIDN'T MATTER WHETHER I GOT A TIP OR NOT. I WOULD SPIT IT OUT, MY RESENTMENT— THAT HE DARES MAKE ME FEEL I'M OPERATING ONLY FOR A TIP.

HE'D ASK FOR HIS CHECK. MAYBE HE'S GOING TO SIGN IT. HE'D TAKE A VERY LONG TIME AND HE'D MAKE ME STAND THERE, "LET'S SEE NOW, WHAT DO YOU THINK I OUGHT TO GIVE YOU?" HE WOULD NOT LET GO OF THAT MOMENT. AND YOU KNEW IT. YOU KNEW HE MEANT TO DEMEAN YOU. HE'S HOLDING THE CHANGE IN HIS HAND, OR IF HE'D SIGN, HE'D FLOURISH THE PEN AND WAIT. THESE ARE THE TIMES I REALLY GET ANGRY. I'M NOT RETICENT. SOMETHING WOULD COME OUT. THEN I DIDN'T REALLY CARE. "GODDAMN, KEEP YOUR MONEY!"

THERE ARE CONVENTIONEERS, WHO LEAVE THEIR LOVELY WIVES OR THEIR BAD WIVES. THEY APPROACH YOU AND SAY, "ARE THERE ANY HOT SPOTS?" "WHERE CAN I FIND GIRLS?" IT IS, OF COURSE, FIRST DIRECTED AT YOU.

I DON'T MEAN THAT AS A COMPLIMENT, 'CAUSE ALL THEY'RE LOOKING FOR IS FEMALES. THEY'RE NOT LOOKING FOR COMPANIONSHIP OR CONVERSATION. I AM QUITE ADEPT AT UNDERSTANDING THIS.

I THINK I'M INTERESTING ENOUGH THAT SOMEONE MAY JUST WANT TO TALK TO ME. BUT I WOULD PHILOSOPHIZE THAT WAY. AFTER ALL, WHAT IS LEFT AFTER YOU TALK? THE HOURS HAVE GONE BY AND I COULD BE HOME RESTING OR READING OR STUDYING GUITAR, WHICH I DO ON OCCASION.

I WOULD SAY, "WHAT ARE YOU GOING TO OFFER ME? DRINKS?" AND THEN I'D POINT TO THE BAR, "I HAVE IT ALL HERE." HE'D LOOK BLANK AND THEN I'D SAY, "A MAN? IF I NEED A MAN, WOULDN'T YOU THINK I'D HAVE ONE OF MY OWN? MUST I WAIT FOR YOU?"

IF YOU BECOME TOO GOOD A WAITRESS, THERE'S JEALOUSY. THEY DON'T COME IN AND SAY, "WHERE'S THE BOSS?" THEY'LL ASK FOR DOLORES. IT DOESN'T MAKE A HIT. THAT MAKES IT ROUGH.

SOMETIMES YOU SAY, AW HELL, WHY AM I TRYING SO HARD? I DID GET AN ULCER. MAYBE THE THINGS I KEPT TO MYSELF WERE TWISTING ME.

IT'S NOT THE CUSTOMERS, NEVER THE CUSTOMERS. IT'S INJUSTICE. MY DAD CAME FROM ITALY AND I THINK OF HIS BROKEN ENGLISH— *INJOOST.* HE HATED INJUSTICE. IF YOU HATE INJUSTICE FOR THE WORLD, YOU HATE MORE THAN ANYTHING INJUSTICE TOWARD YOU.

LOYALTY IS NEVER APPRECIATED, PARTICULARLY IF YOU'RE THE TYPE WHO DOESN'T LIKE SMALL TALK AND ARE NOT THE TYPE WHO MAKES REPORTS ON YOUR FELLOW WORKER. THE BOSS WANTS TO FIND OUT WHAT IS GOING ON SURREPTITIOUSLY.

IN OUR SOCIETY TODAY YOU HAVE INFORMERS EVERYWHERE. THEY'VE INFORMED ON COOKS, ON COWORKERS. "OH SOMEONE WASTED THIS." THEY WOULD SAY I'M TALKING TO ALL THE CUSTOMERS. "I SAW HER CARRY SUCH-AND-SUCH OUT. SEE IF SHE WROTE THAT ON HER CHECK." "THE SALAD LOOKED LIKE IT WAS A DOUBLE SALAD."

I DON'T GIVE ANYTHING AWAY. I JUST GIVE MYSELF. INFORMERS WILL MANUFACTURE THINGS IN ORDER TO MAKE THEIR JOB WORTHWHILE. THEY'RE NOT SURE OF THEMSELVES AS WORKERS. THERE'S ALWAYS SOMEONE WHO WANTS YOUR STATION, WHO WOULD BE PRETENDER TO THE CROWN. IN LIFE THERE IS ALWAYS SOMEONE WHO WANTS SOMEBODY'S JOB.

I'D GET INTOXICATED WITH GIVING SERVICE. PEOPLE WOULD ASK FOR ME AND I DIDN'T HAVE ENOUGH TABLES. SOME OF THE GIRLS ARE STANDING AND DON'T HAVE CUSTOMERS. THERE IS RESENTMENT. I FEEL SELF-CONSCIOUS. I FEEL A SENSE OF GUILT. IT CRAMPS MY STYLE. I WOULD LIKE TO SAY TO THE CUSTOMER, "GO TO SO-AND-SO." BUT YOU CAN'T DO THAT, BECAUSE YOU FEEL A SENSE OF LOYALTY.

SO YOU WOULD RUSH, GET TO YOUR CUSTOMERS QUICKLY. SOME DON'T CARE TO DRINK AND STILL THEY WAIT FOR YOU. THAT'S A COMPLIMENT.

THERE IS PLENTY OF TENSION. IF THE COOK ISN'T GOOD, YOU FIGHT TO SEE THAT THE CUSTOMERS GET WHAT YOU KNOW THEY LIKE. YOU HAVE TO USE DIPLOMACY WITH COOKS, WHO ARE ALWAYS DANGEROUS. (LAUGHS.) THEY'RE MADMEN. (LAUGHS.) YOU HAVE TO BE THEIR FRIEND. THEY BETTER LIKE YOU.

AND YOUR BARTENDER BETTER LIKE YOU TOO, BECAUSE HE MAY DO SOMETHING TO THE DRINK. IF YOUR BARTENDER DOESN'T LIKE YOU, YOUR COOK DOESN'T LIKE YOU, YOUR BOSS DOESN'T LIKE YOU, THE OTHER GIRLS DON'T LIKE YOU, YOU'RE IN *TROUBLE*.

AND THERE WILL BE CUSTOMERS WHO ARE HYPOCHONDRIACS, WHO FEEL THEY CAN'T EAT, AND I COAX THEM. THEN I HOPE I CAN GET IT JUST THE RIGHT WAY FROM THE COOK. I MAY MIX THE SALAD MYSELF, JUST THE WAY THEY WANT IT.

MAYBE THERE'S A PARTY OF TEN. BIG SHOTS, AND
THEY'D SAY, "DOLORES, I HAVE SPECIAL CLIENTS, DO
YOUR BEST TONIGHT." YOU JUST HOPE YOU HAVE THE
RIGHT COOK BEHIND THE BROILER. YOU REALLY WANT
TO PLEASURE YOUR GUESTS. HE'S SELLING SOME-
THING, HE WANTS THINGS RIGHT, TOO. YOU'RE GIVING
YOUR ALL. HOW DOES THE STEAK LOOK? IF YOU CUT
HIS STEAK, YOU LOOK AT IT SURREPTITIOUSLY.
HOW'S IT GOING?

CARRYING DISHES IS A PROBLEM. WE DO HAVE ACCIDENTS. I SPILLED A
TRAY ONCE WITH STEAKS FOR SEVEN ON IT. IT WAS A BIG, GIGANTIC
T-BONE, ALL SLICED. BUT WHEN THAT TRAY FELL, I WENT WITH IT, AND
NEVER MADE A SOUND, DISH AND ALL (SOFTLY) NEVER MADE A SOUND.
IT TOOK ABOUT AN HOUR AND A HALF TO COOK THAT STEAK. HOW
WOULD I EXPLAIN THIS THING? THAT STEAK WAS SALVAGED. (LAUGHS.)

SOME DON'T CARE.
WHEN THE PLATE IS
DOWN YOU CAN
HEAR THE SOUND.
I TRY NOT TO HAVE
THAT SOUND. I WANT
MY HANDS TO BE
RIGHT WHEN I
SERVE. I PICK UP A
GLASS, I WANT IT
TO BE JUST RIGHT.
I GET TO BE
ALMOST ORIENTAL
IN THE SERVING.
I LIKE IT TO LOOK
NICE ALL THE WAY.

TO BE A
WAITRESS,
IT'S AN *ART*.

I FEEL LIKE A BALLERINA, TOO. I HAVE TO GO BETWEEN THOSE
TABLES, BETWEEN THOSE CHAIRS - MAYBE THAT'S THE REASON
I ALWAYS STAYED SLIM. IT IS A CERTAIN WAY I CAN GO
THROUGH A CHAIR NO ONE ELSE CAN DO. I DO IT WITH AN AIR.
IF I DROP A FORK, THERE IS A CERTAIN WAY I PICK IT UP. I
KNOW THEY CAN SEE HOW DELICATELY I DO IT. I'M ON STAGE.

JUST A WAITRESS. AT THE END OF THE NIGHT I FEEL *DRAINED.*

I THINK A LOT OF WAITRESSES BECOME ALCOHOLICS BECAUSE OF THAT. IN MOST CASES, A WAITER OR WAITRESS DOESN'T EAT. THEY HANDLE FOOD, THEY DON'T HAVE TIME. YOU'LL PICK AT SOMETHING IN THE KITCHEN, MAYBE A PIECE OF BREAD. YOU'LL HAVE A CRACKER, A LITTLE BIT OF SOUP. YOU GO BACK AND TAKE A TEASPOONFUL OF SOMETHING.

THEN MAYBE SIT DOWN AFTERWARDS AND HAVE A DRINK, MAYBE THREE, FOUR, FIVE. AND BARTENDERS, TOO, MOST OF THEM ARE ALCOHOLICS. THEY'D GO OUT IN A GROUP. THERE ARE AFTER-HOUR PLACES. YOU'VE GOT TO GO RELEASE YOUR TENSION. SO THEY GO OUT BEFORE THEY GO TO BED. SOME OF THEM STAY OUT ALL NIGHT.

IT BUILDS AND BUILDS AND BUILDS IN YOUR GUTS. NEAR CRYING. I CAN THINK ABOUT IT – (SHE CRIES SOFTLY.) 'CAUSE YOU'RE *TIRED.* WHEN THE NIGHT IS DONE, YOU'RE TIRED. YOU'VE HAD SO MUCH, THERE'S SO MUCH GOING – YOU *HAD* TO GET IT DONE. THE DREAD THAT SOMETHING WOULDN'T BE RIGHT, BECAUSE YOU WANT TO PLEASE.. YOU HOPE EVERYONE IS *SATISFIED.*

THE NIGHT'S DONE, YOU'VE DONE YOUR ACT. THE CURTAINS CLOSE.

THE NEXT MORNING IS PLEASANT AGAIN.

I TAKE OUT MY BUDGET BOOK, WRITE DOWN HOW MUCH I MADE, WHAT MY BILLS ARE. I'M MANAGING. I WON'T GIVE UP THIS JOB AS LONG AS I'M ABLE TO DO IT. I FEEL OUT OF CONTACT IF I JUST SIT AT HOME. AT WORK THEY ALL CONSIDER ME A **KOOK.** (LAUGHS.) THAT'S OKAY.

NO MATTER WHERE I'D BE, I WOULD MAKE A ROUGH ROAD FOR ME. IT'S JUST ME, AND I CAN'T KEEP STILL. IT HURTS, AND WHAT HURTS HAS TO COME OUT.

POSTSCRIPT- "After sixteen years –that was seven years ago—I took a trip to Hawaii and the Caribbean for two weeks. Went with a lover. The kids saw it—they're all married now. (Laughs.) one of my daughters said, "Act your age." I said, "Honey, if I were acting my age, I wouldn't be walking. My bones would ache. You don't want to hear about my arthritis. Aren't you glad I'm **happy**?"

In the Spotlight

RIP TORN (ACTOR)

He came to the big city from a small town in East Texas. Because of some manner, inexplicable to those who hire actors, he has been declared "troublesome." Though he has an excellent reputation as an actor, he has—to many producers and sponsors a "reputation" as a person:

"I have certain flaws in my make-up...I get angry easily, I get saddened by things easily. I figured, as an actor, I could use my own kind of human machinery. The theater would be the place for my flaws to be my strengths...I can use my feelings at work…But I found out that's not what they want. They want you to be their Silly Putty."
—S.T.

A LOT OF YOUNG ACTORS COME UP AND SAY, "I HAVE RESPECT FOR YOU BECAUSE YOU NEVER SOLD OUT." I'VE SOLD OUT A *LOT* OF TIMES.

WE ALL HAVE TO MAKE ACCOMMODATIONS WITH THE KIND OF SOCIETY WE LIVE IN. WE GOTTA PAY THE RENT. I'VE DONE JOBS I WASN'T PARTICULARLY *PROUD* OF.

I DON'T HAVE ANY CONTEMPT FOR PEOPLE WHO DO COMMERCIALS. I'VE NEVER BEEN *ABLE* TO GET THAT KIND OF WORK.

A FRIEND OF MINE GAVE ME A NAME, SOMEBODY TO SEE. SHE SAID, "YOU'LL HAVE TO SHAVE YOUR BEARD." THIS WAS BEFORE BEARDS AND LONG HAIR WERE "IN."

I SAID, "IT'S ONLY A VOICE-OVER, WHAT DIFFERENCE DOES IT MAKE?"

SO I WENT UP TO READ A BRYLCREEM COMMERCIAL.

"THERE MUST HAVE BEEN *FORTY PEOPLE* IN THE CONTROL BOOTH. THERE ARE USUALLY ABOUT *FIVE*.

"I *DIDN'T* GET THE JOB. THEY CAME TO LOOK AT THE *FREAK*.

"I WENT AROUND AND READ ABOUT THREE OR FOUR COMMERCIALS.

"THEY LIKED WHAT I DID, BUT I NEVER GOT ANY *WORK*."

1

I DON'T KNOW. MAYBE YOU DON'T BOW TO THEM CORRECTLY. IF I COULD LEARN THAT CERTAIN *BOW*, MAYBE I'D TRY IT.

YEARS AGO, IN HOLLYWOOD, SOMEONE SAID, "YOU DON'T UNDERSTAND. THIS TOWN IS RUN ON *FEAR.* YOU DON'T APPEAR TO BE *AFRAID.*"

I WENT TO A PARTY. A BIG PRODUCER GAVE IT...

"IT WAS ALONGSIDE THE POOL. MUST HAVE BEEN 150 PEOPLE THERE. THEY HAD A DIVING BOARD UP IN A TREE."

WHEN I WAS A KID, I COULD DIVE OFF A THING LIKE THAT AND DO A *DOUBLE FLIP.*

YOU NEVER DID THAT IN YOUR WHOLE *LIFE.*

I GUESS I COULD DO IT *NOW.*

THAT COULD BE ARRANGED.

WE MIGHT AS WELL MAKE A BET ON THIS. I'LL BET YOU A *DOLLAR.*

"I SHOULD HAVE BET HIM A *GRAND.*

"ALL THE PEOPLE AT THIS PARTY WATCHED ME.

2

"...I WAS READING A PAN AM COMMERCIAL. THE MAN WHO WROTE IT CAME OUT OF THE CONTROL BOOTH..."

I REMEMBER YOU AROUND THAT POOL IN HOLLYWOOD. YOU THOUGHT YOU WERE PRETTY *BIG* IN THOSE DAYS, DIDN'T YOU?

YOU DON'T *REMEMBER* ME, *DO* YOU?

"I GUESS HE WAS ONE OF THOSE WHO DIDN'T TALK TO ME THAT NIGHT."

I WANT TO TELL YOU THAT *TWENTY LINES* OF THIS COMMERCIAL HAS MORE THOUGHT, MORE ARTISTRY, MORE TIME SPENT...

...MORE *MONEY* SPENT THAN IS SPENT ON YOUR USUAL *BROADWAY PLAY.*

I BELIEVE YOU.

GIVE US A VOICE LEVEL, PLEASE.

PAN AM FLIES TO—

WHEN YOU SAY THAT WORD "PAN AM"—

I'M JUST GIVING YOU A VOICE LEVEL. I'M NOT GIVING YOU A *PERFORMANCE* YET.

"SO I TRIED AGAIN, BUT..."

NOT MUCH BETTER.

"HE JUST WANTED TO *CAVE* MY *HEAD* IN."

DO YOU THINK HE WAS *GETTING EVEN* FOR MY SOCIAL GAFFE?

YOU WORK OUT OF *NECESSITY*, BUT IN YOUR WORK, YOU GOTTA HAVE A LITTLE *ARTISTRY*, TOO.

END

Adapted by DANNY FINGEROTH: writer / BOB HALL: artist / JANICE CHIANG: letterer

He is sixty-five years old, though his appearance and manner are of William Blake's "golden youth."
He has been a tenor saxophone player for forty-seven years. Highly respected among
his colleagues, he is a member of "The World's Greatest Jazz Band."
It is a cooperative venture, jointly owned by the musicians, established jazz men.
"I'm with the young people because they refuse to be brainwashed by the things you and I were
brainwashed by. My father, although he worked hard all his life, was very easy with us. Dad was being
brainwashed by the people in the neighborhood. They'd come in everyday and say, "Why don't
your boys go to work?" so he made the mistake of awakening my brother at seven thirty.
I pretended to be asleep. Dad said, "You're going to get up, go out into the world and get jobs and
amount of something." My brother said, "How dare you wake us up before the weekend?" (Laughs.)
I don't recall ever having seen my father since. (Laughs.)

Bud Freeman, Jazz Musician

I GET UP ABOUT NOON. I WOULD ONLY CONSIDER MYSELF OUTSIDE THE NORM BECAUSE OF THE WAY OTHER PEOPLE LIVE. THEY'RE CONSTANTLY REMINDING ME I'M ABNORMAL. I COULD NEVER BEAR TO LIVE THE DULL LIVES THAT MOST PEOPLE LIVE, LOCKED UP IN OFFICES. I LIVE IN ABSOLUTE FREEDOM. I DO WHAT I DO BECAUSE I WANT TO DO IT. WHAT'S WRONG WITH MAKING A LIVING DOING SOMETHING INTERESTING?

I WOULDN'T WORK FOR ANYBODY. I'M WORKING FOR ME. ODDLY ENOUGH, JAZZ IS A MUSIC THAT CAME OUT OF THE BLACK MAN'S OPPRESSION, YET IT ALLOWS FOR GREAT FREEDOM OF EXPRESSION, PERHAPS MORE THAN ANY OTHER ART FORM. THE JAZZ MAN IS EXPRESSING FREEDOM IN EVERY NOTE HE PLAYS. WE CAN ONLY PLEASE THE AUDIENCE DOING WHAT WE DO. WE HAVE TO PLEASE OURSELVES FIRST.

adapted by **Lance Tooks**

I KNOW A GOOD MUSICIAN WHO WORKED FOR LAWRENCE WELK. THE MAN MUST BE TERRIBLY IN NEED OF MONEY. IT'S REGIMENTED MUSIC. IT DOESN'T SWING, IT DOESN'T CREATE, IT DOESN'T TELL THE STORY OF LIFE. IT'S JUST THE KIND OF MUSIC THAT PEOPLE WHO DON'T CARE FOR MUSIC WOULD BUY.

I'VE HAD PEOPLE SAY TO ME, "YOU DON'T DO THIS FOR A LIVING, FOR HEAVEN'S SAKE?" I WAS SO SHOCKED. I SAID, "WHAT OTHER WAY AM I GOING TO MAKE A LIVING? YOU WANT TO SEND ME A CHECK?" (LAUGHS.) PEOPLE CAN'T UNDERSTAND THAT THERE ARE ARTISTS IN THE WORLD AS WELL AS DRONES.

I ONLY KNOW THAT AS A CHILD I WAS OF A REBELLIOUS NATURE. I SAW LIFE AS IT WAS PLANNED FOR MOST OF US. I DIDN'T WANT ANY PART OF THAT DULL LIFE. I WORKED FOR LORD AND TAYLOR ONCE, NINE TO FIVE. IT WAS TERRIBLY DULL. I LASTED SIX WEEKS. I COULDN'T SEE MYSELF BEING A NINE-TO-FIVE MAN, SAVING MY MONEY, GETTING MARRIED, AND HAVING A BIG FAMILY? GOOD GOD, WHAT A WAY TO LIVE!

I KNEW WHEN I WAS EIGHT YEARS OLD THAT I WASN'T GOING TO AMOUNT TO ANYTHING IN THE BUSINESS WORLD. (LAUGHS.) I WANTED MY LIFE TO HAVE SOMETHING TO DO WITH ADVENTURE, SOMETHING UNKNOWN, SOMETHING INVOLVED WITH A FREE LIFE, SOMETHING TO DO WITH WONDER AND ASTONISHMENT. I LOVED TO PLAY- THE FACT THAT I COULD EXPRESS MYSELF IN IMPROVISATION, THE UNPLANNED.

I LOVE TO PLAY NOW MORE THAN EVER, BECAUSE I KNOW A LITTLE MORE ABOUT MUSIC. I'M INTERESTED IN DEVELOPING THEMES AND PLAYING SOMETHING CREATIVE. LIFE NOW IS NOT SO DIFFICULT. WE WORK SIX MONTHS A YEAR. WE LIVE AROUND THE WORLD. AND WE DON'T HAVE TO WORK IN NIGHT CLUBS NIGHT AFTER NIGHT AFTER NIGHT.

PLAYING IN NIGHT CLUBS, I USED TO THINK, WHEN ARE WE GOING TO GET OUT OF HERE? MOST AUDIENCES WERE DRUNK AND YOU TENDED TO BECOME LAZY. AND IF YOU WERE A DRINKER YOURSELF, *THERE* WENT YOUR MUSIC. THIS IS WHY SO MANY GREAT TALENTS HAVE DIED OR GOTTEN OUT OF IT. THEY HATED THE MUSIC BUSINESS. I WAS LUCKY- NOW I'M SIXTY-FIVE- IN HAVING PLAYED FORTY-SEVEN YEARS.

IF JAZZ MUSICIANS HAD BEEN GIVEN THE CHANCE WE IN THIS BAND HAVE TODAY- TO THINK ABOUT YOUR WORK AND NOT HAVE TO PLAY ALL HOURS OF THE NIGHT, FIVE OR SIX SETS- *GOD!* OR RADIO STATION WORK OR COMMERCIAL JINGLE WORK- THE GUYS MUST LOATHE IT. I DON'T THINK THE JAZZ MAN HAS BEEN GIVEN A FAIR CHANCE TO DO WHAT HE REALLY WANTS TO DO, TO WORK UNDER CONDITIONS WHERE HE'S NOT TREATED LIKE A SLAVE, NOT SUBJECT TO THE MUSIC BUSINESS, WHICH WE'VE LOATHED ALL OUR LIVES.

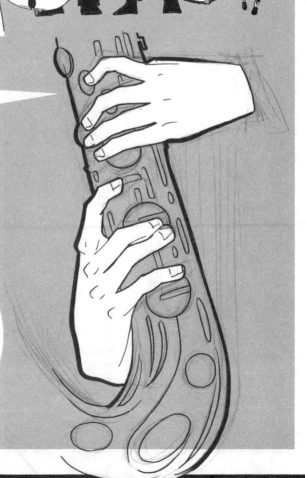

I'VE COME TO LOVE MY WORK. IT'S MY WAY OF LIFE. JAZZ IS A LUXURIOUS KIND OF MUSIC. YOU DON'T PLAY IT ALL DAY LONG. YOU DON'T PLAY IT ALL NIGHT LONG. THE BEST WAY TO PLAY IT IS IN CONCERTS. YOU'RE ON FOR AN HOUR OR TWO AND YOU GIVE IT EVERYTHING YOU HAVE, YOUR *BEST*. AND THE AUDIENCE IS SOBER. AND I'M NOT IN A HURRY TO HAVE THE NIGHT FINISH. PLAYING NIGHT CLUBS, IT WAS ENDLESS.

IF YOU'RE A CREATIVE PLAYER, SOMETHING MUST HAPPEN, AND IT WILL. SOME SORT OF MAGIC TAKES PLACE, YET IT ISN'T MAGIC. HUNDREDS OF TIMES I'VE GONE TO WORK THINKING, OH MY GOD, I HATE TO THINK OF PLAYING TONIGHT. IT'S GOING TO BE AWFUL. BUT SOMETHING ON THAT GIVEN NIGHT TAKES PLACE AND I'M EXCITED BEFORE IT'S OVER. DOES THAT MAKE SENSE? IF YOU HAVE THAT KIND OF NIGHT, YOU'RE NOT AWARE OF THE TIME, BECAUSE OF THIS THING THAT HITS YOU.

THERE'S BEEN A LOT OF UNTRUTHS TOLD ABOUT IMPROVISATION. MEN JUST DON'T GET UP ON THE STAGE AND IMPROVISE ON THINGS THEY'RE NOT FAMILIAR WITH. TRUE IMPROVISATION COMES OUT OF HARD WORK. WHEN YOU'RE PRACTICING AT HOME, YOU WORK ON A THEME AND YOU WORK OUT ALL THE POSSIBILITIES OF THAT THEME. SINCE IT'S IN YOUR HEAD, IT COMES OUT WHEN YOU PLAY. YOU DON'T GET OUT ON THE STAGE AND JUST IMPROVISE, NOT KNOWING WHAT THE HELL YOU'RE DOING. IT DOESN'T WORK OUT THAT WAY. ALWAYS JUST BEFORE I PLAY A CONCERT, I GET THE DAMN HORN OUT AND PRACTICE. NOT SCALES, BUT LOOK FOR CREATIVE THINGS TO PLAY. I'LL PRACTICE TONIGHT WHEN I GET HOME, BEFORE I GO TO WORK. I CAN'T WAIT TO GET AT IT.

I PRACTICE BECAUSE I WANT TO PLAY BETTER. I'VE NEVER BEEN TERRIBLY INTERESTED IN TECHNIQUE, BUT I'M INTERESTED IN FACILITY. TO FEEL COMFORTABLE, SO WHEN THE IDEA SHOOTS OUT OF MY HEAD I CAN FINGER IT, MANIPULATE IT.

SOMETHING INTERESTING HAPPENS. YOU'LL HEAR A PHRASE AND ALL OF A SUDDEN YOU'RE THROWN INTO A WHOLE NEW INSPIRATION. IT DOESN'T HAPPEN EVERY NIGHT. BUT EVEN IF I HAVE A TERRIBLE NIGHT AND SAY, "OH I'M SO TIRED, I'LL GO TO SLEEP AND I'LL THINK OF OTHER THINGS," THE MUSIC'LL COME BACK. I WASN'T TOO HAPPY ABOUT GOING TO WORK LAST NIGHT BECAUSE I WAS TIRED. IT WAS A DRAG. BUT TODAY I FEEL GOOD. GONNA GO HOME AND BLOW THE HORN NOW FOR A WHILE.

PRACTICING IS NO CHORE TO ME. I LOVE IT. I REALLY DO LOVE TO PLAY THE HORN ALONE. THEY CALL ME THE NARCISSISTIC TENOR, (LAUGHS.) BECAUSE I PRACTICE BEFORE THE MIRROR. ACTUALLY I'VE LEARNED A GREAT DEAL LOOKING IN THE MIRROR AND PLAYING. THE DREAM OF ALL JAZZ ARTISTS IS TO HAVE ENOUGH TIME TO THINK ABOUT THEIR WORK AND PLAY AND TO DEVELOP.

THERE WAS A TIME WHEN I WAS ALTOGETHER BORED WITH MY WORK. ABSOLUTELY. I QUIT PLAYING FOR A YEAR. I MET A VERY RICH WOMAN. WE WENT TO SOUTH AMERICA TO LIVE. WE HAD A HOUSE BY THE SEA. I NEVER REALIZED HOW ONE COULD BE SO RICH, SO UNHAPPY, AND SO BORED. IT FRIGHTENED ME. BUT I DID NEED THE YEAR OFF. WHEN I CAME BACK, I FELT FRESH.

Wish I Weren't Here

THE OTHER TIME WAS WHEN I HAD A BAND OF MY OWN. I HAD A NAME, SO I NO LONGER WORKED FOR BIG BANDS. I WAS EXPECTED TO LEAD ONE OF MY OWN. BUT I CAN'T HANDLE OTHER PEOPLE. IF I HAVE A GROUP AND THE PIANIST, LET'S SAY, DOESN'T LIKE MY PLAYING, I CAN'T PLAY. I DON'T SEE HOW THESE BAND LEADERS DO IT. I CAN'T STAND ANY KIND OF RESPONSIBILITY OTHER THAN THE MUSIC ITSELF. I HAVE TO WORK AS A SOLOIST. I CAN BE THE CUSTODIAN ONLY OF MY OWN BEING AND THINKING.

I HAD THIS BAND AND THE GUYS WERE LATE ALL THE TIME. I DIDN'T WANT TO HAVE TO HASSLE WITH THEM. I DIDN'T WANT TO MISTREAT THEM, SO I SAID, "FELLAS, SHOULD WE QUIT?" I WOULDN'T LET THEM GO AND STAY ON MYSELF. WE WERE GOOD FRIENDS. I'D SAY I'D QUIT IF THEY DIDN'T COME IN ON TIME. THEY STARTED TO COME IN ON TIME. BUT I WASN'T A LEADER. I USED TO STAND BY IN THE BAND! A BIT TO THE SIDE. (LAUGHS.) NOW WE HAVE A COOPERATIVE BAND. SO I HAVE A FEELING I'M WORKING FOR MYSELF.

I DON'T KNOW IF I'LL MAKE IT, BUT I HOPE I'LL BE PLAYING MUCH BETTER FIVE YEARS FROM NOW. I OUGHTA, BECAUSE I KNOW A LITTLE BIT MORE OF WHAT I'M DOING. IT TAKES A LIFETIME TO LEARN HOW TO PLAY AN INSTRUMENT. WE HAVE A LOT OF SENSATIONAL YOUNG PLAYERS COME UP- OH YOU HEAR THEM FOR SIX MONTHS, AND THEN THEY DROP OUT. THE KID OF THE MOMENT, THAT'S RIGHT.

REAL TALENT TAKES A LONG TIME TO MATURE, TO LEARN HOW TO BRING WHAT CHARACTER YOU HAVE INTO SOUND, INTO YOUR PLAYING. NOT THE INSTRUMENT, BUT THE STYLE OF MUSIC YOU'RE TRYING TO CREATE SHOULD BE AN EXTENSION OF YOU. AND THIS TAKES A WHOLE LIFE.

I WANT TO PLAY FOR THE REST OF MY LIFE. I DON'T SEE ANY SENSE IN STOPPING. WERE I TO LIVE ANOTHER THIRTY YEARS- THAT WOULD MAKE ME NINETY-FIVE -WHY NOT TRY TO PLAY? I CAN JUST HEAR THE CRITICS, "DID YOU HEAR THAT WONDERFUL NOTE OLD MAN FREEMAN PLAYED LAST NIGHT?" (LAUGHS.)

BUD FREEMAN

AS BEN WEBSTER SAYS, "I'M GONNA PLAY THIS GODDAMNED SAXOPHONE UNTIL THEY PUT IT ON TOP OF ME." IT'S BECOME DEARER TO ME AFTER HAVING DONE IT FOR FORTY-SEVEN YEARS. IT'S A THING I NEED TO DO.

STEVE HAMILTON (BASEBALL PLAYER)

He is a well-traveled relief pitcher, having been with the Washington Senators, New York Yankees, San Francisco Giants, and Chicago Cubs. "I live in the foothills of the Cumberland Mountains. Morehead, Kentucky, is a town of only four thousand. I'm not a hero there 'cause everybody knows everybody."
—S.T.

"I THINK OF ALL THE TIME I STOOD OUTSIDE MY HOUSE IN CHARLESTOWN, INDIANA...

WAP

"...A TWO-TONE BRICK WALL...

WAP

"...AND I THREW A BASEBALL WHERE THE DIFFERENT COLORS MET.

WAP

"I HIT IT OVER AND OVER AGAIN..."

1

AUGUST 1971.

AGE IS VERY IMPORTANT IN BASEBALL.

MOST OF US IN BASEBALL WHO ARE *THIRTY* ARE CONSIDERED *OLD MEN*.

I DON'T *FEEL* OLD, BUT IN BASEBALL, I'M *ANCIENT*.

TO BE PERFECTLY HONEST WITH YOU...

"...I'M READY TO QUIT. I'M LOSING THE DESIRE.

"I'M TIRED OF TRAVELING. I'M TIRED OF THE HOURS.

"AND I'M LOSING THE ZEST. WHEN THIS HAPPENS, IT'S TIME TO LEAVE.

"FOR A DAY GAME, I GET TO THE PARK ABOUT TEN. WE SIGN ANYWHERE FROM ONE TO TWO DOZEN BASEBALLS EVERY DAY.

"WHEN I WAS WITH THE YANKEES, WE SIGNED *SIX DOZEN* EACH DAY!

"WE USED TO *HATE* THAT.

"PEOPLE IN THE FRONT OFFICE HAVE FRIENDS THEY WANT TO GIVE THEM TO.

"I DON'T KNOW WHERE ALL THOSE BALLS GO.

"*SIX DOZEN* A DAY! *EIGHTY-ONE* DAYS!

"THAT'S A *LOT* OF BASEBALLS!"

I'VE NEVER BEEN A BIG STAR. I'VE NEVER DONE ANYTHING OUTSTANDING.

I FEEL I'VE BEEN AS GOOD AS I CAN BE WITH THE EQUIPMENT I HAVE.

WHETHER GUYS ADMIT IT OR NOT, I THINK MOST OF THEM FEEL GOOD WHEN THEY'RE RECOGNIZED. I THINK THAT'S PART OF THE GAME.

I PLAYED WITH *MICKEY MANTLE* AND NOW I'M PLAYING WITH *WILLIE MAYS.* PEOPLE ALWAYS RECOGNIZE *THEM.* BUT FOR PEOPLE TO RECOGNIZE *ME...!*

ONCE YOU START GETTING RECOGNIZED, IT BECOMES IMPORTANT TO YOU. WHEN I CAME OVER TO THE NATIONAL LEAGUE, NOBODY ASKED FOR MY AUTOGRAPH BECAUSE I HAD GRAY HAIR.

IT STARTED TO *BOTHER* ME. I PUT STUFF ON MY HAIR AND IT WENT SORT OF MEDIUM-BROWN. BUT I DON'T LIKE IT AND I'M LETTING IT GROW OUT.

KI-IK!

"NO MATTER *HOW* HARD I TRY, I COULD NEVER BE A *SANDY KOUFAX.*

"BUT IF I CAN BE AS GOOD AS *STEVE HAMILTON,* I FEEL I'VE BEEN SUCCESSFUL."

WAP

END

Adapted by DANNY FINGEROTH: writer/ BOB HALL: artist/ JANICE CHIANG: letterer

Behind a Desk

"It bothers me when the boss is there. When the boss is around, if he sees you reading a paper or something, it grates on him. That's the part of the job I dislike most--having to look busy."

DON'T YOU HAVE ANYTHING BETTER TO DO?

"One of the older guys was telling me how amazing he found it that I would sit there totally oblivious to the boss and read a paper. That ran against his ethic. I think there's too much of an attitude that work has to be shitty."

YOU DON'T HAVE TO MAKE YOURSELF SUFFER.

"I noticed someone talking on the phone the other day, one of the older guys. He said he was at the office. It dawned on me that when a guy says 'I'm at the office', it means 'I don't dirty my hands.' He wasn't at work--he was 'at the office'. It really blew my mind. I don't think I've used that phrase in my life. I say 'I'm at work.'"

WHATAYA DOIN'?

I'M WORKING.

"I'm not afraid of the boss. I think he's sort of afraid of me. He's afraid of the younger people at work because they're not committed to the job. The older person, who's got his whole life wrapped up in the organization, the boss can keep him from getting a promotion or a raise. If he makes a little mistake, he'll freak out, because his whole career is dangling there."

OH MY GOD! I SCREWED UP!

"The boss doesn't have that power over us so the tables are sort of reversed. We have power over him, because he doesn't know how to persuade us. We do the job and we do it fine, but he doesn't know why. The older guys work because they want to get ahead, but he doesn't know why we do."

THESE KIDS DON'T SEEM TO CARE ABOUT ANYTHING!

"I can't figure him out. It's a weird mixture of condescension, trying to be a nice guy-- 'Wouldn't you do this?'--and trying to be stern. Part of it comes out of his own fear. He doesn't realize younger people resent this. I object to seeing this guy as my father. I'd rather see him as some kind of equal, or boss."

WOULD YOU MIND WORKING A COUPLE OF EXTRA HOURS TODAY?

"Older people, he tells them what to do, and they do it, because that's the way it is. But he never feels sure the younger people are going to do it. They want to know why. Nobody refuses to do anything, but we want to know why."

CAN YOU EXPLAIN THAT, SIR?

"If there's a lull in the work the kids'll go into the main office and they'll sleep on the couches. The big boss complained to my boss and my boss asked if I would pass the word along not to sleep on the couches anymore. I said 'Why?' If there's nothing to do and it's the middle of the night, and people want to grab a nap..."

JUST DO ME A FAVOR AND PASS IT ON.

"He said, 'Well, that's what the boss said.' I just told him 'No, I wouldn't feel right telling them. You'll have to tell them yourself.' It's really stupid. If the couch is there and somebody's tired, he should lay down on the floor to keep this guy's couch neat for next Monday?"

SORRY... I PREFER NOT TO.

T.JABAN

David Reed Glover

WE'RE IN THE OFFICES OF REED GLOVER AND COMPANY, A BROKERAGE FIRM ON LA SALLE STREET, ALONG CHICAGO'S FINANCIAL DISTRICT.

"MY FATHER WAS A FOUNDING PARTNER. THERE ARE TWELVE PARTNERS. WE HAVE ABOUT TWENTY SALESMEN, WHO ALSO HANDLE THE CUSTOMERS' ACCOUNTS. THESE SALESMEN ARE OTHERWISE KNOWN AS CUSTOMERS' MEN. OUR FIRM WAS FOUNDED IN 1931 BY MY FATHER, REED GLOVER. HE HAD BEEN A BANKER IN A DOWNSTATE TOWN. HE FELT AN INVESTMENT FIRM WAS NEEDED TO SERVE THE SMALL COMMUNITY BANKS. NOW THERE ARE FIFTEEN THOUSAND BANKERS, MOSTLY IN THE MIDDLE STATES, WHO RECEIVE OUR LETTERS. AFTER HAVING BEEN ON THE LIST FOR FORTY YEARS, MANY OF THEM GET AROUND TO CALLING US. I'D SAY WE'RE MEDIUM SIZED".

I'M FORTY YEARS OLD. I STARTED IN THE SECURITIES BUSINESS IN 1954, THE ONLY JOB OUTSIDE THE ARMY I'VE HAD. I BELIEVED WE WERE IN A NEW ERA. I THOUGHT THE FOUNDING PARTNERS OF MY FIRM WERE HAMPERED BY A DEPRESSION-ERA PSYCHOLOGY, THAT THEY DIDN'T UNDERSTAND THERE COULD NO LONGER BE A SEVERE COLLAPSE IN STOCK PRICES. THE SENIOR BROKERS WERE CONSIDERED OLD FOGIES AND STODGY FOR THEIR UNWILLINGNESS TO GO ALONG WITH SOME OF THIS NEW THINKING. THERE HAS BEEN A GREAT CHASTENING AMONG YOUNGER MEN. WHAT HAPPENED IN 1968 AND 1969 IS THAT A GREAT MANY LARGE FIRMS OVER-EXPANDED. WORSE THAN THAT, THEY RECOMMENDED STOCKS WHICH WERE UNSOUND. I'M TALKING NOW ABOUT THE CONGLOMERATES. YOU'VE HEARD ABOUT THE FOUR SEASONS NURSING HOMES, ABOUT ELECTRONIC STOCKS. THIS BECAME THE RAGE. WHEN THE DOWNTURN OCCURRED IN '69 AND '70, MANY OF THESE FIRMS WENT OUT OF BUSINESS. THEY FORGOT THAT THERE REALLY ISN'T A NEW ERA. THE BUSINESS CYCLE IS NOT GOING TO VANISH. YOU MUST BE PREPARED FOR ADVERSITY AS WELL AS PROSPERITY. I REALIZE NOW THERE ARE CERTAIN PRINCIPLES THAT MUST BE ADHERED TO.

"THERE HAVE BEEN MANY TIMES OF PERSONAL QUESTIONING ABOUT MY OCCUPATION. THE WORST TIME CAME WHEN I APPROACHED THE MAGIC MARK OF FORTY (LAUGHS). DURING THAT TIME WE WERE IN THE HEART OF THE EAR MARKET (LAUGHS), AND THIS IS A HIGHLY EMOTIONAL BUSINESS. WHEN THE MARKET IS ON ITS WAY UP, YOU HAVE A FEELING OF WELL-BEING AND FULFILMENT, OF CONTRIBUTING TO THE WELFARE OF OTHERS. WHEN THE MARKET IS GOING DOWN, THIS IS A RATHER UNFORTUNATE LINE TO BE IN. WHEN YOU'RE DEALING WITH AN INDIVIDUAL'S MONEY IT'S A TERRIFIC RESPONSIBILITY".

THE INDIVIDUAL OF MEANS IS EXPOSED TO SO MANY PEOPLE IN THE BROKERAGE BUSINESS THAT IT'S QUITE A COMPLIMENT TO HAVE HIM TURN TO YOU FOR INVESTMENT SERVICE. THE RULE I'VE ALWAYS GONE BY IS THAT I EXPECT TO HAVE MY BROTHER-IN-LAW'S ACCOUNT AND MY ROOMMATE IN COLLEGE. BUT IT SEEMS EVERYBODY HAS A ROOMMATE IN COLLEGE OR A BROTHER-IN-LAW WHO'S IN THIS BUSINESS. SO I DON'T REALLY USE MY SOCIAL ACQUAINTANCES FOR PURPOSES OF BUSINESS. MY CLOSEST FRIENDS ARE WITH MANY OF THE BROKERAGE FIRMS. AT SOCIAL GATHERINGS WE DON'T DISCUSS THE MARKET, OTHER THAN IN AN AMUSING RATHER THAN A SERIOUS WAY.

I'M AMAZED HOW RARELY THE INDIVIDUAL CUSTOMER WILL FIND FAULT WITH THE BROKER. ALONG WITH THAT, THERE'S NO WRITTEN CONTRACT IN OUR BUSINESS. IF THE STOCK GOES DOWN, THE CUSTOMER'S WORD IS HIS ONLY PLEDGE.

THEY ALL PAY. THIS IS AN HONORABLE BUSINESS.

"WHEN YOU'RE DEALING WITH A PERSON'S MONEY AND INVESTMENTS, YOU DEAL WITH HIS HOPES AND AMBITIONS AND DREAMS. MORE PEOPLE ARE BECOMING SOPHISTICATED IN UNDERSTANDING THAT THEY CAN ACTUALLY OWN PART OF A CORPORATION LIKE GENERAL MOTORS SIMPLY BY PLACING AN ORDER FOR AN INTANGIBLE ITEM LIKE A STOCK CERTIFICATE".

HELLO, DAVID, I'LL LIKE TO PURCHASE...

IT'S QUITE EASY TO LOOK AROUND AND SAY THIS IS A PARASITICAL BUSINESS. ALL YOU'RE DOING IS RAKING OFF YOUR CUT FROM THE PRODUCTIVITY OF OTHERS. THAT IS, I THINK, AN ERRONEOUS VIEW. FRANKLY, I'VE WRESTLED WITH THAT. IT COMES DOWN TO THIS: THE BASIS OF THIS COUNTRY'S STRENGTH AND PROSPERITY IS THE FINEST ECONOMIC SYSTEM THAT'S EVER BEEN DEVISED, WITH ALL ITS INEQUITIES AND IMPERFECTIONS. OUR SYSTEM DEPENDS ON A FREE EXCHANGE OF PUBLICY OWNED ASSETS, AND WE'RE PART OF THE PICTURE.

"IF THERE WERE NO STOCK MARKET, I THINK THE ECONOMY WOULD BE STIFLED. IT WOULD PREVENT THE GROWTH OF OUR COMPANIES IN MARKETING THE SECURITIES THEY NEED FOR THEIR EXPANSION. LOOK AT COMMONWEALTH EDISON. IT CAME OUT JUST THE OTHER DAY WITH A MILLION SHARES. WITHOUT THE STOCK MARKET, THE COMPANIES WOULDN'T BE ABLE TO INVEST THEIR CAPITAL AND GROW. THIS IS MY LIFE AND I COUNT MYSELF VERY FORTUNATE TO BE IN THIS WORK. IT'S FULFILLING".

AH, ANOTHER QUITE SATISFACTORY DAY.

Harvey Pekar & Pablo G. Callejo

Beryl Simpson
AIRLINE RESERVATIONIST
BY HARVEY PEKAR & EMILY NEMENS · 2008

My job as a reservationist was very routine, computerized. I hated it with a passion; getting sick in the morning, going to work feeling "OH MY GOD! I've got to go to work..."

Oh, God, I don't know if I can make it today...

I was on the Astrojet desk. It has an unlisted number for people who travel all the time. This was a special desk for people who spend umpteen millions of dollars traveling with the airlines. They spend ten thousand dollars a month, a hundred thousand a month, depending on the company.

Uh huh, uh huh.

ASTROJET

I was dealing with the same people every day.

This is so-and-so from such-and-such a company, and I want a reservation to New York and return, first class.

That was the end of the conversation.

They brought in a computer called *SABRE*. It's like an electronic typewriter. It has a memory drive and you can retrieve information—forever.

FLIGHT INFO...

SABRE was so expensive, everything was geared to it. SABRE's down, SABRE's up.

...SABRE this and SABRE that, everything was SABRE.

PAGE①

READY SET RING!

hello? ...got a go! whew! Oh no!

ASTROJET

The last three or four years on the job were horrible. The computer had arrived. They monitored you and listened to your conversation. If you were a minute late, it went in your file. I had a horrible attendance record — ten letters in my file, a total of ten minutes.

With SABRE being so valuable, you were allowed no more than three minutes on the phone. You had twenty seconds, busy-out time it was called, to put information into SABRE. Then you had to be available for another phone call. It was almost like a production line. The casualness, the informality that had been there previously were no longer there.

You took thirty minutes for your lunch, not thirty-one. If you got a break, you took ten minutes, not eleven.

RX KEANER

When I was with the airlines, I was taking eight tranquilizers a day. I came into this business, which is supposed to be one of the most hectic, and I'm down to three a day. Even my doctor remarked "Your ulcer is healed, it's going away." With the airlines I had no free will. I was just part of this stupid computer.

I remember when I went to work for the airlines, they said:

Welcome Thanks

RULES

ASTROJET

YOU WILL: eat, drink, and sleep airlines. There's no time in your life for ballet, theater, music, anything. My supervisor told me that.

Another agent and I were talking about going to the ballet or something. He overheard us and said we should be talking about work. When you get airline people together they'll talk about planes. That is all they talk about.

That and Johnny Carson. They are TV-oriented people.

He just cracks me up!

 I had so much more status when I was working for the airlines than I have now. I was always introduced as Beryl Simpson who works for the airline. Now I'm reduced to plain old Beryl Simpson. I found this with boyfriends. I know one who never dates a girl with a name. He never dates a Judy, he never dates a Joan. He dates a stewardess, or a model. He picks girls for the glamour of their jobs. He never tells you their names. When I was with the airlines, I was introduced by my company's name. Now I'm just plain old everyday me, thank God.

Yeah, she works for the airline.

Whoop-dee-doo.

I have no status in this man's eyes, even though I probably make twice as much as some of the ones he's proud of. If I'd start to talk about some of the stocks I hold, he'd be impressed. This is true of every guy I ever dated when I was working on the airlines. I knew I had a dumb, stupid, ridiculous, boring job, and these people were glamorizing it. "Oh, she works for the airlines." Big deal.

The Small Town Times

5¢   SMALL TOWN, USA • SUNDAY, AUGUST 5, 1970

Beryl Simpson, airline worker, just back from exotic place.

FARMERS SAY THEY SAY...

When I used to go back home, the local paper would run my picture and say that I work for the airlines and that I had recently returned from some exotic trip or something. Romance.

 A lot of times we get airline stewardesses into our office who are so disillusioned. We'd like to frame their application when we get a bright-eyed, starry-eyed kid of eighteen who wants a job in the airlines. Big as life disillusionment. We want to say "It's not what its cracked up to be, girlie."

If a girl's a stewardess, she might as well forget it after twenty-six. They no longer have compulsory retirement, but the girls get in a rut at that age. A lot of them start showing the rough lives they've lived.

I'm twenty-seven, what will I do with myself?

RING!

Appearance

SAM MATURE, BARBER

He has been a barber for forty-three years. For twenty-one years he has owned a shop at the same locale, an office building in Chicago's Loop.

A master barber may have a couple of other barbers that are better barbers than he is, but they call him the master because he's the boss.

Long hair is nothin' new. We had some fancy haircuts them days the same as we do today. I did a bit of musicians and they had long hair. But not like the hippie. I have no objections as long as they keep it clean, neat, a little light trim.

But you know what gets me? A fella's got a son in college, he's got long hair, which he's in style. Here's the old man, he wants to get long hair. And he's the average age fella, in the fifty age bracket. He wants to look like his son. Now that to me is ridiculous. Happens quite often. The fella'll come in and he'll say, "I'm gonna let my hair grow, Sam, because my daughter or my wife..." Daughters and wives tell husbands how to cut their hair. The guy's been married for twenty-five years. I don't see the sense in him changing.

You're gonna do what?

We still like what they call the he-man cut. Businessman haircut. Not all this fancy stuff. It's not here to stay.

It hurt the barber quite a bit. I know about nine barbers went out of business in this area alone. A man used to get a haircut every couple weeks. Now he waits a month or two, some of 'em even longer than that.

We used to have customers that'd come in every Friday. Once a week, haircut, trim, everything. Now the same fella would come in every two months. That's the way it goes.

We used to have five chairs here. Now there's only three or two. We used to have a manicurist here that works five days a week. Now she works one day a week.

A lot of people would get manicured and fixed up every week. Most of these people retired, moved away, or they passed away. It's all on account of long hair.

You take the old-timers, they wanted to be presentable and they had to make a good appearance in their office.

Now people don't seem to care too much. You take some of our old-timers, they still take shampoo and a hair tonic and get all fixed up. But if you take the younger generation today, if you mention, "Do you want something in your hair?" they feel you insulted them. I had one fella here not too long ago, I said, "Do you want your hair washed?" He said, "What's the matter? Is it dirty?" (laughs) A young guy. An older person wouldn't do that.

Is it dirty?

In the city of Chicago, a haircut's three dollars with the exception of the hair stylin' shops. They charge anything they want. It runs as high as twelve dollars. We don't practice it, the three of us can do it but we don't recommend it. We have to charge a man so much money. I don't think it's considerate, that kind of price for a haircut.

How much?

Still $3.00

In stylin', you part his hair different, you cut his hair different. Say you got a part and you don't want no part. You comb it straight back, you're changing his style. Say his part's on the right side. All right, you change his style, you put the part on the left side. Then you wash his hair and you cut him down and redress his hair over again. That's hair stylin'. I never went for that myself.

I'm gonna comb your hair straight back, OK?

Yeah, OK.

When I came here twenty-one years ago we had a separate chair here in the little room, in which I cut all ladies' hair. We'd run about six or seven or eight cuts a day in women's hair. I won second prize cutting ladies' hair, which was back in 1929. The windblown haircut. Their hair was all combed forward. It was like a gust of wind hits you in the back of the head, and blew your hair forward. Today young girls don't know what it is. I think it's a lot easier than cutting men's hair. They're less trouble, too.

What'll it be today, Mam?

Most of your new barbers today, actually there isn't too many takin' it up. Take these barber colleges. It used to be three, four hundred students. Not any more. You get four, maybe six, there. Not only that, the tuition has gone up so high. It cost me $160. Now it would run you six hundred dollars or better. Young barbers today, unless they go in for hair styling, it isn't enough money in it.

I'm not workin' for no thirty bucks less.

So many of them, they get disgusted for the simple reason that it takes too long to be a barber. When I took up barberin' it took six months. Today you have to apprentice three years before you can get your license. You work for a lot less — about thirty dollars less than a regular barber would get.

You can't think of other things while you're working. You concentrate on the man's hair or you'd better be talkin' to him about whatever he wants to talk about. A barber, he has to talk about everything — baseball, football, basketball, anything that comes along. Religion and politics most barbers stay away from (laughs). Very few barbers that don't know sports. A customer'll come in, they'll say, "What do you think of the Cubs today?" Well, you gotta know what you think.

What do you think of the Cubs today?

Oh, they're doin' swell.

You say, "Oh, they're doin' swell today." You have to tell 'em. Fans today in sports are terrific, hockey, all those things. That counts in bein' a barber, you gotta know your sports. They'll come in, "What did you think of that fight last night?" Lotta sports barbers has to watch on TV or hear about it or read about it. You gotta have somethin' to tell him. You have to talk about what he wants to talk about.

I'm tellin' ya, they don't make 'em like Rocky Marciano any more.

Amen t'that.

Usually I do not disagree with a customer. If there is something that he wants me to agree with him, I just avoid the question (laughs). This is about a candidate, and the man he's speaking for is not the man you're for and he asks you, "What do you think?" I usually have a catch on that. I don't let him know which party I'm with. The way he talks, I can figure out which party he's from, 'cause you might mention the party he's against. And that's gonna hurt business.

McCarthy has it right, there's too many commies in government t'day.

Amen t'that.

I'll disagree on sports. Fans are all different. TV plays a good role, especially during ball games, real good. All the shops should have TV, because the customer, he wants to look at something, to forget his office work, forget the thing he has in his mind that he has to do.

Runner on first, two outs.

Watchin' TV relaxes his mind from what he was doin' before he came in the shop.

A lot of people sit down and relax. They don't want to have anything to do, just sit there and close their eyes. Today there is less closin' their eyes.

We had customers at one time, if they couldn't go to sleep, they wouldn't get a haircut.

Customers call me by my first name — Sam. I have customers twenty years old that call me Sam. I call the customer Mister. I never jump to callin' a man by his first name unless he tells me himself, "Why don't you call me Joe." Otherwise I call him Mister.

You can call me Shane.

About tips. Being a boss, sometimes they figure they don't have to tip you. They don't know that the boss has to make a living same as anybody else. Most of your master barbers, they don't bank on it, but they're glad to get whatever they get. If a man, through the kind heart of his, wants to give me something, it's all right. It's pretty hard to keep a person from tipping. They tip a bellhop, they tip a redcap, they tip a waiter.

Here's something for your trouble.

If bosses in these shops would agree to pay the barber more, I'd say ninety percent wouldn't do it. They'd rather the customer help pay this barber's salary by tipping him. I'm in favor of not tipping. I'd rather pay the man ten dollars more a week than have him depend on that customer. This way he knows he's got that steady income. In the old days you kind of depended on tips because the salary was so small. If you didn't make the extra ten dollars a week in tips you were in bad shape.

C'mon, man, tip me,

I'll tell ya, by tipping that way it made me feel like a beggar. A doctor, you don't give him a tip. He's a professional man. You go to the dentist, you don't give him a tip because he fixed your tooth. Well a barber is a professional man too, so I don't think you should tip him.

That's a'right, keep it. I'm a professional man.

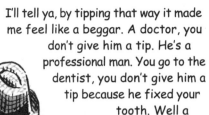

When I leave the shop I consider myself not a barber any more. I never think about it. When a man asks me what I do for a living I try to avoid that question. I figure it's none of his business. There are people who think a barber is a nobody. If I had a son I'd want him to be more than just a barber.

What's gonna happen when you retire?

They're gonna be just another barber short.

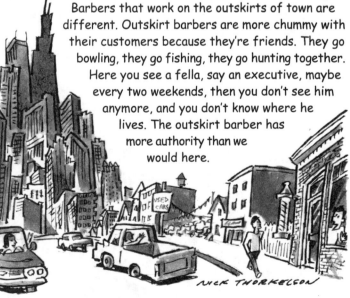

Barbers that work on the outskirts of town are different. Outskirt barbers are more chummy with their customers because they're friends. They go bowling, they go fishing, they go hunting together. Here you see a fella, say an executive, maybe every two weekends, then you don't see him anymore, and you don't know where he lives. The outskirt barber has more authority than we would here.

NICK THORKELSON

"Do you have a favorite tune? Here's an oldie." He plays "As Time Goes By."
The piano bar is fairly crowded. The drinking is casual. It is early evening at the downtown hotel.
Once it was a favorite gathering place for the city's sporting crowd, politicians,
and strangers looking for action. It will be razed this year to make way for a modern high rise.
He started here in 1952. he refers to a mutual friend, who has since died. "Chet and I began
the whole thing. The first piano bar was in this hotel. Now every tavern and saloon has one."
There is a jukebox in the room. Its loudness envelops all during the piano breaks.
He works five nights a week, from five-thirty to "round midnight. If there's a crowd,
I keep going. I might play many hours in a row. I take a break when it's empty."
There are frequent phone calls for him, interrupting the conversation.

Hots Michaels, Bar Pianist

PIANO PLAYING IS INCIDENTAL TO THIS PLACE. IT'S KIND OF BACKGROUND MUSIC FOR TALKING. BUSINESSMEN TALKING DEALS. OUT-OF-TOWN VISITORS. OCCASIONALLY YOU GET SOME PEOPLE INTERESTED IN HEARING A CERTAIN TYPE OF SONG, AND YOU ENTERTAIN THEM. I NEVER TOOK ANY LESSONS. I PLAY STRICTLY BY EAR. I'M LUCKY I CAN READ TITLES. (LAUGHS)

OVER THE YEARS I GET TO KNOW PEOPLE. THEY'LL HIT THE PIANO BAR AND WE'LL TALK BACK AND FORTH. A SECOND GROUP WILL MOVE IN, STRANGERS. THEY MIGHT BE FROM SMALL TOWNS AND THEY WANT TO KNOW WHAT'S HAPPENING. YOU HAVE CLOSE CONTACT WITH PEOPLE. THIS PETRIFIES SOME PIANO PLAYERS, SO THEY PLAY WITH BANDS. I NEVER PLAYED WITH A BAND BECAUSE I WASN'T QUALIFIED.

adapted by **Lance Tooks**

LATE BUSINESS IS A THING OF THE PAST. PEOPLE DON'T STAY DOWN AS LATE AS THEY USED TO AFTER WORK. THE LOCAL PEOPLE WILL HAVE THEIR DRINKS AND GO HOME. AT ONE TIME THEY STAYED DOWN FIVE, SIX HOURS. AND THEY DON'T COME DOWN LIKE THEY USED TO. THEY HAVE PLACES OUT IN THE SUBURBS. AND I THINK THERE'S A LITTLE BIT OF FEAR. I'LL SEE PEOPLE CHECK INTO THE HOTEL, COME DOWN AND SIT AROUND THE PIANO BAR. THEY'RE REALLY AFRAID TO LEAVE THE HOTEL. IT'S THE STRANGEST THING. MYSELF, I FEEL VERY SAFE. EVIDENTLY MY WORK AT THE PIANO BAR WILL BE ENDED. NOTHING IS FOREVER.

I HATE TO SEE IT END. I'LL DREAD THE DAY IT COMES, BECAUSE I ENJOY THE ACTION. I ENJOY PEOPLE. IF I WERE SUDDENLY TO INHERIT FOUR MILLION DOLLARS, I GUARANTEE YOU I'D BE PLAYIN' PIANO, EITHER HERE OR AT SOME OTHER PLACE. I CAN'T EXPLAIN WHY. I WOULD MISS THE FLOW OF PEOPLE IN AND OUT.

YOU'RE KIND OF A LISTENING BOARD HERE. SOMETIMES THEY TELL ME THINGS I WISH THEY'D KEEP TO THEMSELVES. PERSONAL, MARRIAGE PROBLEMS, BUSINESS. I GET ABOUT TWENTY CALLS A NIGHT. A WIFE LOOKING FOR A HUSBAND TO BRING SOMETHING HOME. IN A CUTE WAY SHE'S TRYING TO FIND OUT IF HE'S HERE OR SOMEPLACE ELSE. IF HE DOESN'T SHOW UP IN AN HOUR, *I'LL* BE HEARING. (LAUGHS.) I COVER UP CONSTANTLY. THEY TELL ME THINGS I'D JUST AS SOON NOT KNOW. (LAUGHS.)

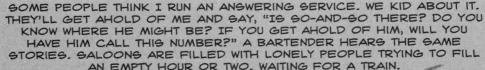

SOME PEOPLE THINK I RUN AN ANSWERING SERVICE. WE KID ABOUT IT. THEY'LL GET AHOLD OF ME AND SAY, "IS SO-AND-SO THERE? DO YOU KNOW WHERE HE MIGHT BE? IF YOU GET AHOLD OF HIM, WILL YOU HAVE HIM CALL THIS NUMBER?" A BARTENDER HEARS THE SAME STORIES. SALOONS ARE FILLED WITH LONELY PEOPLE TRYING TO FILL AN EMPTY HOUR OR TWO. WAITING FOR A TRAIN.

THERE'S ONLY A FEW THINGS THAT SEPARATE YOU FROM THE MASSES OF WORKERS. THROUGH THIS BUSINESS I HAVE MET SOME DIGNITARIES. WHERE ELSE COULD A PIANO PLAYER MEET PRESIDENT TRUMAN OR BOB HOPE OR PEOPLE LIKE THAT? I'D NEVER DO IT IF I WERE A STEAM FITTER OR A PLUMBER.

THERE'S NOTHING WRONG WITH THEIR LINE OF WORK. THEY PROBABLY MAKE MORE THAN A PIANO PLAYER. EXCEPT I HAPPEN TO BE WHERE PEOPLE GATHER. IT'S A GOOD FEELING. WE'RE FIGHTING FOR A LITTLE BIT OF STATUS, ONE WAY OR ANOTHER.

EVERY MINUTE OF MY LIFE I DEAL WITH A DRINKING PUBLIC. I'M NOT KNOCKING IT, THEY PAY MY SALARY. BUT YOU HAVE TO TREAT THEM A CERTAIN WAY AFTER THEY HAVE A FEW MARTINIS. THEY CHANGE THAT RAPIDLY. IT DOESN'T BOTHER ME UNLESS THEY GET ROUGH. IF HE OFFENDS SOMEBODY AROUND THE BAR, SOME WILD VULGARITY, I GET UP AND GET HIM OUT. JUST BY BEING NICE. MOST PEOPLE YOU CAN TALK TO. IT'S MUCH MORE DIFFICULT WITH A WOMAN WHO IS DRINKING. SHE CAN BE DIFFICULT. YOU CAN'T PUT YOUR HANDS ON HER.

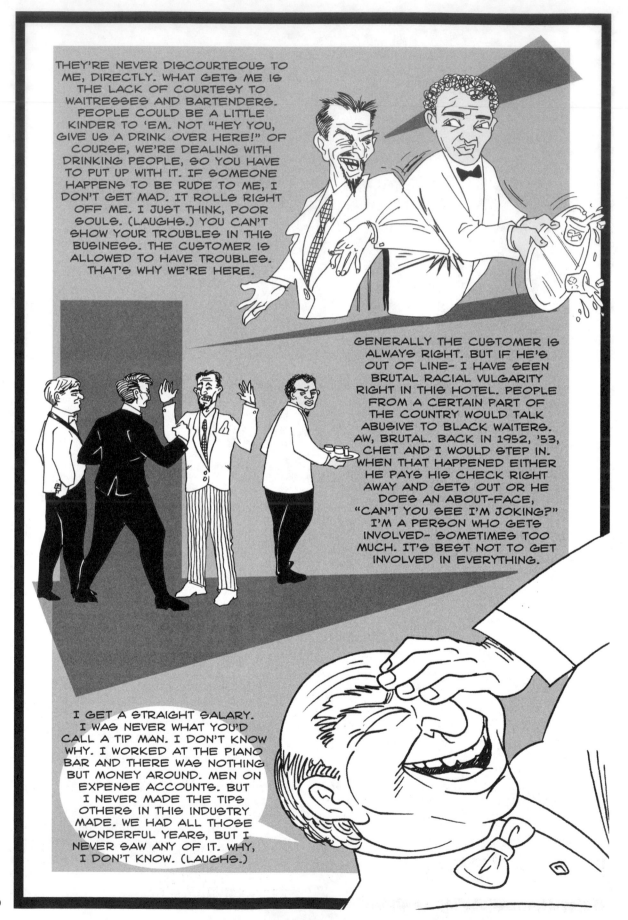

THEY'RE NEVER DISCOURTEOUS TO ME, DIRECTLY. WHAT GETS ME IS THE LACK OF COURTESY TO WAITRESSES AND BARTENDERS. PEOPLE COULD BE A LITTLE KINDER TO 'EM. NOT "HEY YOU, GIVE US A DRINK OVER HERE!" OF COURSE, WE'RE DEALING WITH DRINKING PEOPLE, SO YOU HAVE TO PUT UP WITH IT. IF SOMEONE HAPPENS TO BE RUDE TO ME, I DON'T GET MAD. IT ROLLS RIGHT OFF ME. I JUST THINK, POOR SOULS. (LAUGHS.) YOU CAN'T SHOW YOUR TROUBLES IN THIS BUSINESS. THE CUSTOMER IS ALLOWED TO HAVE TROUBLES. THAT'S WHY WE'RE HERE.

GENERALLY THE CUSTOMER IS ALWAYS RIGHT. BUT IF HE'S OUT OF LINE— I HAVE SEEN BRUTAL RACIAL VULGARITY RIGHT IN THIS HOTEL. PEOPLE FROM A CERTAIN PART OF THE COUNTRY WOULD TALK ABUSIVE TO BLACK WAITERS. AW, BRUTAL. BACK IN 1952, '53, CHET AND I WOULD STEP IN. WHEN THAT HAPPENED EITHER HE PAYS HIS CHECK RIGHT AWAY AND GETS OUT OR HE DOES AN ABOUT-FACE, "CAN'T YOU SEE I'M JOKING?" I'M A PERSON WHO GETS INVOLVED— SOMETIMES TOO MUCH. IT'S BEST NOT TO GET INVOLVED IN EVERYTHING.

I GET A STRAIGHT SALARY. I WAS NEVER WHAT YOU'D CALL A TIP MAN. I DON'T KNOW WHY. I WORKED AT THE PIANO BAR AND THERE WAS NOTHING BUT MONEY AROUND. MEN ON EXPENSE ACCOUNTS. BUT I NEVER MADE THE TIPS OTHERS IN THIS INDUSTRY MADE. WE HAD ALL THOSE WONDERFUL YEARS, BUT I NEVER SAW ANY OF IT. WHY, I DON'T KNOW. (LAUGHS.)

IT MIGHT BE A SORT OF INDEPENDENCE I HAVE. SOMETIMES PEOPLE FEEL THEY WOULD OFFEND BY TIPPING ME. HERE'S YOUR CITY GUY SITTING AT THE PIANO AND HE'S DRESSED RATHER WELL. HE SEEMS TO BE GETTING ALONG WITH THE CROWD. MAYBE THEY FEEL HE DOESN'T NEED IT. MOST OF THE PEOPLE IN TOWN, THE REALLY BIG SPENDERS, THE SPORTY CLASS, I KNEW TOO WELL. THEY STARTED TIPPING ME, BUT THE FIRST THING YOU KNOW I'M THAT PERSON'S FRIEND AND THAT'S THE END OF THE TIP. I KNOW PIANO PLAYERS THAT KEEP ALOOF. THEY'LL WALK OUT OF THE ROOM ON A BREAK. THEY STAY AWAY FROM PEOPLE ON THEIR OWN TIME. IT'S GOOD PSYCHOLOGY.

I COULDN'T DO THAT. NATURALLY ANYONE WOULD WANT TO MAKE A LITTLE EXTRA MONEY, BUT IT WASN'T THE TARGET IN MY LIFE. I WAS NEVER A HUSTLER. THERE'S A WAY OF HUSTLING PEOPLE FOR TIPS. YOU CAN PUT A BOWL ON THE PIANO, PUT A FEW DOLLARS IN IT. THERE'S ALSO A VERBAL WAY. A FELLA IS HITTING YOU FOR A FEW TUNES. HE KEEPS IT UP. THERE'S WAYS OF KIDDING HIM, "GOD, THAT'S A FIVE-DOLLAR NUMBER, THAT ONE." BUT IT JUST DOESN'T RUN IN ME. IF THEY WANT TO GIVE IT TO ME, FINE. IF THEY DON'T, ALL RIGHT. THEY'RE GONNA GET THE SAME ACTION.

I PLAY ALONG WHETHER IT'S NOISY OR QUIET. IT DOESN'T BOTHER ME IF PEOPLE TALK OR ARE LOUD. IT'S PART OF THE GAME. I NEVER HAD A STRONG EGO. I SOMETIMES WISH I DID. I CAN PLAY ALL THE MELODIES, BUT I'M NOT REALLY A GOOD PIANO PLAYER. I WISH I WERE. I NEVER TOUCH A PIANO UNTIL I WALK IN HERE. I DON'T HAVE A PIANO AT HOME. MY FATHER WAS A TALENTED MUSICIAN. IN OUR HOME THERE WAS ALWAYS A PIANO. EVERYBODY PLAYED, MY FATHER, MY MOTHER, MY BROTHERS, MY SISTER, MYSELF.

142

Cleaning Up

148

NICK SALERNO, GARBAGEMAN

He has been driving a city garbage truck for eighteen years. He is forty-one, married, and has three daughters. He works a forty-hour, five-day week with occasional overtime. He has a crew of three laborers.

I usually get up at five-fifteen.

I get to the city parking lot, you check the oil, your water level, then proceed to the ward yard. You meet the men, we pick up our work sheet.

You get up just like the milkman's horse, you get used to it. If you remember the milkman's horse, all he had to do was whistle and whooshhh! That's it. He just knew where to stop, didn't he?

You pull up until you finish the alley. Usually thirty homes on each side. You have thirty stops in our alley. I have nineteen alleys a week. They're called units.

Sometimes I can't finish 'em, that's how heavy they are, this being an old neighborhood.

I'll sit there until they pick this one stop. You got different thoughts. Maybe you got a problem at home. Maybe one of your children aren't feeling too good. Like my second one. She's got a problem with her homework. Am I doin' the right thing with her? Pressing her a little bit with math.

Or you read the paper. You always daydream.

Some stops there's one can, they'll throw that on, then proceed to the next can. They signal with a buzzer or a whistle or they'll yell. The pusher blade pushes the garbage in. A good solid truckload will hold anywhere from eight thousand to twelve thousand pounds. If it's wet it weighs more.

Years ago you had people burning, a lot of people had garbage burners. You would pick up a lot of ashes. Today most of 'em have converted to gas. In place of ashes, you've got cardboard boxes, you've got wood that people aren't burning anymore.

It's not like years ago, when people used everything.

They're not too economy-wise today.

They'll throw anything away. You'll see whole packages of meat just thrown into the garbage can without being opened. I don't know if it's spoiled from the store or not.

When I first started here I had thirty alleys in this ward. Today I'm down to nineteen. And we got better trucks today. Just the way things are packaged today. Plastic. You see a lot of plastic bottles, cardboard boxes.

We try to give 'em twice-a-week service, but we can't complete the ward twice a week. Maybe I can go four alleys over.

If I had an alley Monday, I might go in that alley Friday.

What happens over the weekend? It just lays there.

After you dump the garbage in the hopper, the sweeper blade goes around to sweep it up, and the push blade pushes it in. This is where you get your sound. Does that sound bother you in the morning? (laughs) Sometimes it's irritating to me. If someone comes up to talk and the men are working in the back, and they press the lever, you can't hear them. It's aggravating, but you get used to it.

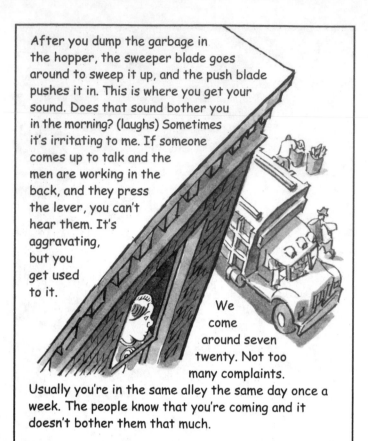

We come around seven twenty. Not too many complaints.

Usually you're in the same alley the same day once a week. The people know that you're coming and it doesn't bother them that much.

Some people will throw, will literally throw, garbage out of the window — right in the alley. We have finished an alley in the morning and that same afternoon it will look like it wasn't even done.

They might have a cardboard carton in the can and garbage all over the alley. People are just not takin' care of it.

You get some people that take care of their property. They'll come out and sweep around their cans.

Other people just don't care or maybe they don't know any better.

Some days it's real nice. Other days when you get off that truck you're tired — that's it! You say all you do is drive but driving can be pretty tiresome — especially when the kids are out of school.

They'll run through a gangway into an alley. That is what you have to watch for. Sitting in that cab you can have a lot of blind spots around the truck. This is what gets you. You watch out that you don't hit any of them.

At times you get aggravated, like your truck breaks down and you get a junk as replacement. This, believe me, you could take home with you.

Otherwise, working here, if there's something on your mind you don't hold anything in. You discuss with these guys. Golf, whatever. One of my laborers just bought a new home and I helped him move some of his small stuff. He's helped me around my house, plumbing and painting.

We've got spotters now, it's new (laughs). They're riding around in unmarked cars. They turn you in for stopping for coffee. I can't see that.

If you have a coffee break in the alley it's just using a little psychology. You'll get more out of them. But if you're watched continually, you're gonna lay down. There's definitely more watching today, because there was a lot of layin' down on the job. Truthfully I'd just as soon put in my eight hours a day as easy as possible. It's hard enough comin' to work.

I got a good crew, we get along together, but we have our days.

If you're driving all day you get tired. By the time you get home, fighting the traffic, you'd just like to relax a little bit. But there's always something around the house, you can get home one night and find your kid threw something in the toilet and you gotta shut your mind and take the toilet apart (laughs).

My wife drives so she does most of the shopping. That was my biggest complaint. So now this job is off my hands, I look forward to the weekends, I get in a little golf.

People ask what I do, I say, I drive a garbage truck for the city. They call you G-man or, "How's business, picking up?" Just the standard.... Or sanitary engineer. I have nothing to be ashamed of. I put in my eight hours. We make a pretty good salary. I feel I earn my money. I can go anywhere I want. I conduct myself as a gentleman anyplace I go.

My wife is happy, this is the big thing. She doesn't look down at me.

They made a crack to my children in school. My kids would just love to see me do something else. I tell'm, "Honey, this is a good job. There's nothing to be ashamed of. We're not stealin' the money. You have everything you need." I don't like my salary compared to anyone else's. I don't like to hear that we're makin' more than a school teacher. A schoolteacher should get more money, but

don't take it away from me.

NICK THORKELSON

Second Chance

NICK LINDSAY

Scripted by Harvey Pekar and Illustrated by Pat Moriarity

Though he lives in Goshen, Indiana, he considers his birthplace "home"--Edisto Island, off the coast of South Carolina. At forty-four, he is the father of ten children; the eldest, a girl twenty-six, and the youngest, a boy one and a half years old.

He is a carpenter as well as a poet, who reads and chants his works on college campuses and at coffeehouses. "This is one of the few times in my life I had made a living at anything but carpentry. Lindsays have been carpenters from right on back to 1755.

Every once and a while, one of em'll shoot off and be a doctor or a preacher or something.* Generally, they've been carpenter-preachers, carpenter-farmers, carpenter-storekeepers, carpenters right on. A man, if he describes himself, will use a verb. What you do, that's what you are. I would say I'm a carpenter.

* His father, Vachel Lindsay, was a doctor as well as a celebrated poet.

I started working steady at it when I was thirteen. I picked up a hammer and went to drive in nails. One man I learned a lot from was a janitor, who didn't risk the ebb and flow of the carpentry trade. You can learn a lot from books about things like this---how nails work, different kinds of wood.

He dropped out of high school. "It's a good way to go. Take what you can stand and don't take any more than that. It's what God put the tongue in your mouth for. If it don't taste right, you spit it out."

Ptui!

Let me tell you where the grief bites you so much. Who are you working for? If you're going to eat, you are working for the man who pays you some kind of wage. That won't be a poor man. The man who's got a big family and who's needing a house, you're not building a house for him. The only man you're working for is the man who could get along without it. You're putting a roof on the man who's got enough to pay your wage.

You see over yonder, shack need a roof. over here you're building a sixty-thousand-dollar house for a man who maybe doesn't have any children. He's not hurting and it doesn't mean much. It's a prestige house. He's gonna up-man, he's gonna be one-up on his neighbor, having something fancier. It's kind of into that machine.

It's a real pleasure to work on it, don't get me wrong. Using your hand is just a delight in the paneling, in the good woods. It smells good and they shape well with the plane. Those woods are filled with the whole creative mystery of things. Each wood has it's own spirit. Driving nails, yeah, your spirit will break against that.

What's gonna happen to what you made? You work like you were kneeling down. You go into Riverside Church in New York and there's no space between the pews to kneel. (laughs.) If you try to kneel down in that church, you break your nose on the pew in front. A bunch of churches are like that. Who kneels down in that church? I'll tell you who kneels. The man kneels who's settin' the toilets in the restrooms. He's got to kneel, that's part of his work. The man who nails the pews to the floor, he had to kneel down. The man who put the receptacles in the walls that turn that I-don't-know-how-many horsepower organ they got in that Riverside Church---that thing'll blow you halfway to heaven right away, POW!---the man who was putting the wire in that thing, he kneeled down. Any work, you kneel down---it's a kind of worship. It's part of the holiness of things, work, yes. Just like drawing breath is. It's necessary. If you don't breathe, you're dead. It's kind of a sacrament, too.

One nice thing about the crafts. You work two hours at a time. There's a ritual to it. It's break time. Then two hours more and it's dinner time. All those are very good times. Ten minutes is a pretty short time, but it's good not to push too hard. All of a sudden it comes up break time, just like a friend knocking at the door that's unexpected. It's a time of swapping tales. What you're really doing is setting the stage for your work.

A craftsman's life is nothing but compromise. Look at your tile here. That's craftsman's work, not art work. Craftsmanship demands that you work repeating a pattern to very close tolerences. You're laying this tile here within a sixteenth. It ought to be within a sixty-fourth of a true ninety degree angle. Theoretically it should be perfect. It shouldn't be any sixty-fourth, it should be 00 tolerance. Just altogether straight on, see? Do we ever do it? No. Look at that parquet stuff you got around here. It's pretty, but those corners. The man has compromised. He said that'll have to do.

They just kind of hustle you a little bit. The compromise with the material that's going on all the time. That makes for a lot of headache and grief. Like lately we finished a house. Well, it's not yet done. Cedar siding, that's material that's got knots in it. That's part of the charm. But it's a real headache if the knots falls out. You hit one of those boards with your hammer sometime and it turns into a piece of Swiss cheese. So you're gonna drill those knots, a million knots, back in. (Laughs.) It's sweet smelling wood. You've got a six-foot piece of a ten-foot board. Throwing away four feet of that fancy wood? Whatcha gonna do with that four feet? A splice, scuff it, try to make an invisible joint, and use it? Yes or no? You compromise with the the material. Save it? Burn it? It's in your mind all the time. Oh sure, the wood is sacred. It took a long time to grow that. It's like a blood sacrifice. It's consummation. That wood is not going to go anywhere else after that.

When I started in, it was like European carpentering. But now, all that's pretty well on the run. You make your joints simply, you get pre-hung doors, you have machine-fitted cabinet work, and you build your house to fit these factory-produced units. The change has been toward quickness. An ordinary American can buy himself some kind of a house because we can build it cheap. So again, your heart is torn. It's good and not so good. Sometimes it has to do with how much wage he's getting. The more wage he's getting, the more skill he can exercise. You're gonna hire me? I'm gonna hang your door. Suppose you pay me five dollars an hour. I'm gonna have to hang that door fast. 'Cause if I don't hang that door fast, you're gonna run out of money before I get it hung. No man can hurry and hang it right.

⑤

I don't think there's less pride in craftsmanship. I don't know about pride. Do you take pride in embracing a woman? You don't take pride in that. You take delight in it. There may be less delight. If you can build a house cheap and really get it to a man that needs it, that's kind of a social satisfaction for you. At the same time, you wish you could have done a fancier job, a more unique kind of a job.

HERE ARE THE KEYS.

But every once in a while there's stuff that comes in on you. All of a sudden something falls into place. Suppose you're driving an eight-penny galvanized finishing nail into this siding. Your whole universe is rolled onto the head of that nail. Each lick is sufficient to justify your life. You say, "Okay, I'm not trying to get this nail out of the way so I can get onto something important. There's nothing more important. It's right there." And it goes--POW! It's not getting that nail in that's in your mind. It's hitting it--hitting it square. hitting it straight. Getting it how. That one lick.

If you see a carpenter that's alive to his work, you'll notice that about the way he hits a nail. He's not going (imitates machine gun rat-tat-tat-tat)..trying to get the nail down and out of the way so he can hurry up and get another one. Although he may be working fast, each lick is like a separate person that he's hitting with his hammer. It's like as though there's a separate friend of his that one moment. And when he gets out of it, here comes another one. Unique, all by itself. Pow! But you gotta stop before you get that nail in, you know? That's fine work. Hold the hammer back, and just that last lick, don't hit it with your hammer, hit it with a punch so you won't leave a hammer mark. Rhythm.

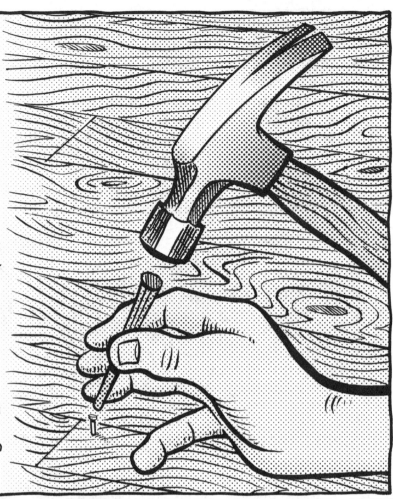

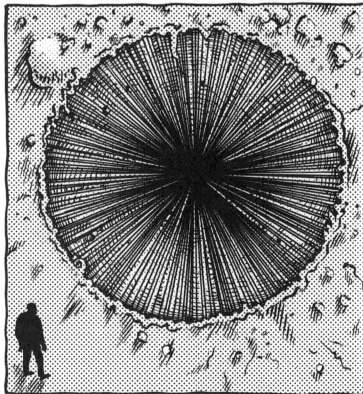

I worked at an H-bomb plant in South Carolina. My work was building forms. I don't think the end product bothered me so much, 'cause Judgement Day is not a thing.... (Trails off.) It doesn't hang heavy on my heart. It might be that I should be persuaded it was inappropriate...They got that big old reactor works with the heavy water and all that. This heavy equipment runs there day and night, just one right after another, going forty miles an hour, digging that big old hole halfway to hell. They build themselves a highway down there, just to dig that hole.

⑦

Now you're gonna have to build you a building, concrete and steel. You ship in a ready-mixed plant just for that building. A pump on the hill. It starts pumping concrete into the hole. It's near about time for the carpenters. We're building forms for the first floor of that thing. I was the twenty-four-hundredth-and-some-odd carpenter hired at the beginning. That's how big it was. There was three thousand laborers. Each time we built one of these reactors, there would be a whole town to support it. We built a dozen or so towns in this one county.

We all understood we were making H-bombs and tried to get it done before the Russians built theirs, see? That's what everybody thought, it was one of those great secret jobs where you had guards at the gates, barbed wire around the place, spies, all that kind of foolishness.

Some people call it the hard lard belt, some call it the Bible belt. Mostly just farmers who stepped from behind the plow, who had tenants or were tenants themselves. It was a living wage in that part of the country for the first time since the boll weevil had been through. And boy, you can't downrate that. It seems like the vast comedy of things when a Yankee come and got us to build their H-bomb, part of the fine comedy that she should come and give us the first living wage since the War of Northern Aggression-for this.

In Bloomington, Indiana, I saw a lot of women make their living making bombs. They had a grand picnic when they built the millionth bomb. Bombs they're dropping on people. And the students came to demonstrate against the bombs. Maybe these women see no sense in what they're doing, but they see their wages in what they're doing...

Some people will say, "I'm a poet. I'm better than you. I'm different. I'm a separate kind of species." It doesn't seem to me poetry is that way. It seems like mockin' birds sing and there's hardly ever a mockingbird that doesn't sing. It's the same way with poetry, it just comes natural to 'em, part of what we're made for. It's the natural utterance of living language. I say my calling is to be a carpenter and a poet. No contradiction.

(Chants) Work's quite a territory. Real work and fake work. There's fake work, which is the prostitution. There is the magic of payday, though. You'll say, "Well, if you get paid for your work, is that prostitution?" No indeed. But how are you gonna prove it's not? A real struggle there. Real work, fake work, and prostitution. The magic of payday. The groceries now heaped on the table and the new-crop wine and store-bought shirts. That's what it says, yes.

PAT McRIARITY

Looking After Each Other
(From Cradle to Grave)

GARY BRYNER

LORDSTOWN LOCAL UAW PRESIDENT

HE'S **TWENTY-NINE**, GOING ON **THIRTY**. HE IS PRESIDENT OF LOCAL 1112, UAW (**UNITED AUTO WORKERS**). ITS MEMBERS ARE **EMPLOYED** AT THE **GENERAL MOTORS** ASSEMBLY PLANT IN **LORDSTOWN**, **OHIO**. LORDSTOWN IS A **CROSSROADS**; PEOPLE HAVE **MIGRATED** THERE FROM CITIES **AROUND** IT.

ART BY
GARY DUMM

IT'S THE **MOST** AUTOMATED, **FASTEST** LINE IN THE **WORLD**.

AFTER GRADUATING FROM HIGH SCHOOL I GOT A **JOB** WHERE MY FATHER WORKED, IN **REPUBLIC STEEL**. IN **FOUR** YEARS I DABBLED WITH THE UNION, WAS A **STEWARD**. I WAS THE **MOST** VERSATILE GUY THERE: **STARTED** ON THE **TRACK GANG**, TO THE **FORGING** DEPARTMENT, AND THEN A **MILLWRIGHT'S** HELPER UNTIL I WAS **LAID OFF**. SPENT **THREE** YEARS AT ANOTHER FACTORY AND REALLY GOT **INVOLVED** IN THE **UNION THERE**...

...IN 1966 I CAME **HERE** TO **GENERAL MOTORS** AT **LORDSTOWN**.

SOMEONE SAID **LORDSTOWN** IS THE **WOODSTOCK** OF THE **WORKINGMAN**. THERE ARE **YOUNG** PEOPLE WHO HAVE THE **MOD** LOOK, **LONG** HAIR, BIG **AFROS**, BEADS, YOUNG GALS. THE **AVERAGE AGE** IS AROUND **TWENTY-FIVE**. I'M A **YOUNG UNION PRESIDENT**, BUT I'M AN **OLD MAN** IN MY **PLANT**.

SIXTY-SIX, WHEN THEY **OPENED** THE COMPLEX FOR **HIRING**, THERE WAS NO **VEGA** IN MIND. WE BUILT A "B" BODY – THE BIG **FAMILY CAR**.

I TOOK ON A **FOREMAN'S** JOB. THEY PUT **30** OF US IN A **MOCK** ARBITRATION CLASS WHILE WE WERE **TRAINING**. ALL THE PEOPLE WERE **COMPANY** PEOPLE: THE UMPIRE, THE ATTORNEYS AND THE GUY TO BE **DISCHARGED**. I WAS THE **ONLY** FOREMAN-TO-BE TO VOTE HIM **INNOCENT**.

YOU THINK HE'S INNOCENT?!

THE OTHERS JUST WANTED TO **PLEASE** THE COMPANY PEOPLE. I TOOK **OFF** THE SHIRT AND **TIE**, SAYING:

THANK YOU, BUT **NO THANK** YOU...

ALL FOREMEN WEAR SHIRTS AND **TIES**. THEY'VE BECOME SOMEWHAT **LIBERAL** NOW AT **GENERAL MOTORS**...

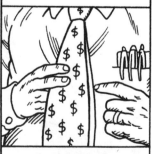

...**FOREMEN** CAN WEAR **COLORED** SHIRTS AND **ANY** KIND OF **TIE**.

I WENT **BACK** AS AN ASSEMBLY **INSPECTOR** – UTILITY. I WAS ABLE TO GET AROUND AND **TALK** TO A **LOT** OF PEOPLE. PEOPLE BEING PRESSURED...FORCED TO **RUN**. IT WAS A **MAIL-FISTED** APPROACH BY **MANAGEMENT** BECAUSE **EVERYBODY** WAS NEW.

...LET'S JOIN THE UNION!

THE **WAY** THEY TREATED US – MANAGEMENT **MADE** MORE **UNION** PEOPLE IN 1966 AND 1967 THAN THE UNION COULD HAVE **THOUGHT** OF MAKING.

WHEN THE **PLANT** FIRST OPENED, IT **WASN'T** YOUNG PEOPLE THEY DREW FROM. IT WAS PEOPLE WHO GAVE **UP** JOBS TO **COME** TO **GM** BECAUSE IT WAS **NEW**. IT WAS AN **ATTRACTIVE** THING TO BE ONE OF THE **FIRST THOUSAND** HIRED. I **THOUGHT** OF IT AS **SECURITY.**

LORDSTOWN ASSEMBLY

GM

UAW LOCAL 1112

OTHER PEOPLE DIDN'T WANT TO COME IN AND WORK THE **SECOND** SHIFT OR TAKE **LESSER** PAYING JOBS, BECAUSE THEY HAD ALREADY **ESTABLISHED** THEMSELVES SOMEWHERE **ELSE** AND **WOULDN'T** STAND IN **LINE** REPETITIVELY DOING A JOB, NOT BEING ABLE TO **GET AWAY.** SO THAT'S WHEN **KIDS** GOT HIRED RIGHT **OUT** OF HIGH SCHOOL. BUT THEY **WOULDN'T** PUT UP WITH IT **EITHER.**

THAT WAS **1967** AND SOON THEY HAD **SPED** UP THE LINE. THEY'D STARTED OUT AT **SIXTY** CARS AN **HOUR.** THERE WAS A **LOT** OF EMPLOYMENT **THEN.** NOW, IN '72, THERE **ISN'T.** PEOPLE GET A JOB **HERE,** THEY **KEEP** IT, BECAUSE THERE'S **NO PLACE** ELSE.

MPLOYMENT FFICE

I **DON'T** GIVE A **SHIT** WHAT ANYBODY SAYS, IT WAS **BORING, MONOTONOUS WORK.**

A GUY COULD BE THERE **EIGHT** HOURS AND THERE WAS **SOME OTHER BODY** DOING THE **SAME** JOB OVER AND OVER, ALL **DAY** LONG, ALL **WEEK** LONG, ALL **YEAR** LONG. **YEARS.** YOU COUNT THE **SPOTS,** THE SAME **COUNT,** THE SAME **JOB,** JOB **AFTER** JOB **AFTER** JOB. IT'S **GOT** TO DRIVE A GUY **NUTS.**

SO **WHAT** HAPPENED? A GUY **FACED UP** TO THE FACTS...HE HAD TO HAVE SOME **TIME**. THE **BEST** WAY IS TO **SLOW DOWN** THE PACE. HE MIGHT WANT TO OPEN A BOOK, SMOKE A CIGARETTE, WALK TWO OR THREE STEPS AWAY TO GET A DRINK OF WATER OR TO **TALK** TO THE GUY NEXT TO HIM. HE THOUGHT HE WASN'T OBLIGATED TO DO **MORE** THAN HIS **NORMAL** SHARE. ALL OF A SUDDEN IT **MATTERED** TO HIM WHAT WAS **FAIR**.

THE **YOUNG** GUY **BELIEVES** HE HAS SOMETHING TO **SAY** ABOUT WHAT HE **DOES**. HE DOESN'T BELIEVE THAT WHEN THE FOREMAN **SAYS** IT'S RIGHT THAT IT'S RIGHT. HE DOESN'T ASK FOR MORE **MONEY**. HE SAYS, "I'LL **WORK** AT A NORMAL PACE, SO I DON'T GO HOME TIRED AND SORE, A PHYSICAL **WRECK**..."

"...I WANT TO KEEP MY **JOB** AND KEEP MY **SENSES**."

MY DAD WAS A **FOREMAN** IN A PLANT. HIS JOB WAS TO **PUSH** PEOPLE, TO **PRODUCE**. HE QUIT **THAT** AND WENT BACK INTO A STEEL MILL. HE WORKED ON THE **INCENTIVE**. THE **HARDER** YOU WORK, THE MORE MONEY YOU MAKE. MY FATHER **WASN'T** A STRONG UNION **ADVOCATE**, HE WAS THERE TO MAKE **MONEY**.

THE ALMIGHTY **DOLLAR** IS NOT THE **ONLY** THING IN MY ESTIMATION. THERE'S MORE TO IT – **HOW** I'M TREATED. WHAT I HAVE TO **SAY** ABOUT WHAT I **DO**, **HOW** I DO IT. THE REASON **MIGHT** BE THAT THE **DOLLAR'S HERE** RIGHT NOW. IT **WASN'T** IN MY FATHER'S **YOUNG** DAYS.

I CAN CONCENTRATE ON THE **SOCIAL** ASPECTS, MY **RIGHTS**. AND I'M ABLE TO STAND UP AND SPEAK UP FOR **ANOTHER** GUY'S RIGHTS. FIGHTING **EVERY** DAY OF MY LIFE. AND I **ENJOY** IT.

GUYS IN PLANTS **NOWADAYS**, THEIR INCENTIVE IS **NOT** TO WORK HARDER. IT'S TO **STOP** THE JOB TO THE POINT WHERE THEY CAN HAVE **LAX** TIME: MAYBE TO **THINK**, OPEN A PAPER, READ A PARAGRAPH, **DO** HIS JOB... KEEPING HIMSELF OCCUPIED **OTHER** THAN BEING **JUST** THAT **ROBOT** THEY'VE **SCHEDULED** HIM TO BE.

WHEN **GENERAL MOTORS ASSEMBLY DIVISION** CAME TO **LORDSTOWN**, THEY TRIED TO TAKE NEWSPAPERS **OFF** THE LINE. THEIR IDEA IS TO CUT **COSTS**, BE **MORE** EFFICIENT, TAKE THE **WASTE** OUT OF WORKING, AND ALL THAT **JAZZ**. THAT'S WHY THE **GUYS** LABELED GMAD: "GOTTA MAKE ANOTHER DOLLAR."

IN **1970** CAME THE **VEGA**. THEY WERE FIGHTING **FOREIGN IMPORTS**. THEY WERE GOING TO MAKE A SMALL **COMPACT** THAT GETS **GOOD MILEAGE**. BUT WITH THE **VEGA**, A **MUCH** SMALLER CAR, THEY WERE GOING FROM **SIXTY** AN HOUR TO **ONE HUNDRED** AN HOUR.

SO WITH **THAT**, WE HAD WHAT WERE CALLED **PARAGRAPH 78** DISPUTES. MANAGEMENT SAYS ON **EVERY** JOB YOU SHOULD DO **THIS** MUCH. THE GUY AND THE UNION SAY THAT'S **TOO MUCH** WORK FOR ME IN **THAT** AMOUNT OF TIME, AND WE ESTABLISH **WORK** STANDARDS. PRIOR TO GMAD WE'D HAD AN **AGREEMENT:** THE GUY WHO WAS **ON** THE JOB HAD SOMETHING TO SAY.

WHEN **GMAD** CAME IN, THEY **SAID:**

...HE'S LONG **OVERDUE** FOR **EXTRA** WORK. HE'S **FEATHERBEDDING.***

*GOOFING OFF. LITERALLY **LAYING DOWN** ON THE JOB.

INSTEAD OF HAVING THE GUY **BEND OVER** TO PICK SOMETHING **UP**, IT'S RIGHT AT **WAIST LEVEL**. THIS IS SOMETHING **FORD** DID IN THE **THIRTIES**. TRY TO TAKE **EVERY MOVEMENT** OUT OF THE GUY'S **DAY**, TO MAKE HIM **MORE** EFFICIENT AND **PRODUCTIVE**, LIKE A **ROBOT**.

SAVE A SECOND ON **EVERY** GUY'S **EFFORT**, THEY WOULD, OVER A YEAR, MAKE A **MILLION DOLLARS**.

THEY USE **TIME: STOPWATCHES**. WE **KNOW** IT TAKES SO MANY **SECONDS** TO SHOOT A SCREW. WE KNOW THE GUN **TURNS SO FAST**, THE SCREW'S SO **LONG**, THE HOLE'S SO **DEEP**. OUR ARGUMENT'S BEEN: THAT'S **MECHANICAL**; THAT'S **NOT** HUMAN.

...WE'RE **NOT** ABOUT TO BE **PLACED** IN THE **CATEGORY** OF A **MACHINE**. WHEN **YOU** TALK ABOUT THAT **WATCH**, YOU TALK ABOUT IT FOR A **MINUTE**. WE TALK ABOUT A **LIFETIME**. WE'RE GONNA DO WHAT'S **NORMAL**. AND WE'RE GONNA **TELL** YOU WHAT'S **NORMAL**. WE'LL **NEGOTIATE** FROM **THERE**.

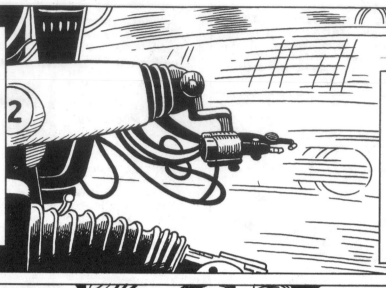

BEFORE THEY TOOK THE **UNIMATES** ON, WE WERE BUILDING **60 CARS** AN HOUR. WHEN WE CAME BACK TO WORK **WITH** THE **UNIMATES**, WE WERE BUILDING **100 CARS** AN HOUR. A UNIMATE IS A **WELDING ROBOT** THAT LOOKS JUST LIKE A **PRAYING MANTIS**.

IT **GOES** FROM SPOT TO SPOT...IT **RELEASES** AND IT **JUMPS** BACK INTO POSITION, **READY** FOR THE **NEXT** CAR. THEY **NEVER** TIRE, SWEAT, COMPLAIN OR **MISS** WORK. OF COURSE, **THEY** DON'T **BUY** CARS. GUESS GM DOESN'T UNDERSTAND THAT **ARGUMENT**.

THERE'S 22, 11 ON EACH SIDE OF THE *LINE*. THEY DO THE WORK OF ABOUT **200** MEN—SO THERE WAS A REDUCTION OF **MEN**. BUT THERE'S SOME **THINKING** ABOUT ASSEMBLING CARS. THERE STILL HAS TO BE **HUMAN BEINGS**.

IF THE GUYS DIDN'T STAND UP AND **FIGHT**, THEY'D BECOME **ROBOTS** TOO. THEY'RE **INTERESTED** IN BEING ABLE TO **SMOKE**, BULLSHIT A BIT, OPEN A BOOK, DAYDREAM EVEN. YOU **CAN'T** DO THAT IF YOU **BECOME** A MACHINE.

ON STRIKE FOR EQUITY

THERE WAS A **STRIKE**. IT CAME AFTER **4 OR 5** MONTHS OF AGITATION BY MANAGEMENT. GMAD TOOK OVER THE PLANT, AND WHERE WE HAD **SETTLED** A GRIEVANCE, THEY VIOLATED 'EM. THEY **LAID OFF** PEOPLE. IT'S A **TWO-SHIFT** OPERATION, SAME JOB, ABOUT **2,800** PEOPLE WITH **1,400** GRIEVANCES. I DON'T THINK GM VISUALIZED THIS KIND OF A **REBELLION**.

THE STRIKE **ISSUE**? WE DEMANDED THE REINSTITUTION OF OUR WORK **PACE** AS IT WAS **PRIOR** TO THE ONSLAUGHT BY GMAD. IN THAT LITTLE **BOOK** OF QUOTES I HAVE:

"THE WORKINGMAN HAS BUT **ONE** THING TO **SELL**, HIS **LABOR**. ONCE HE **LOSES** CONTROL OF **THAT**, HE LOSES **EVERYTHING**."

A **LOT** OF THESE **YOUNG** KIDS UNDERSTAND THIS. THERE'S SOME **MANLINESS** IN BEING ABLE TO **STAND UP** TO THE GIANT.

ASSEMBLY LINE WORKERS ARE THE **LOWEST** ON THE TOTEM POLE WHEN IT COMES TO JOB **FULFILLMENT**. SOME **CORPORATE** GUY SAID, "A **MONKEY** COULD DO THE JOB." THEY COULD CARE **LESS** IF THE **SCREW** GOES IN THE **WRONG** PLACE OR **STRIPS**.

THE CORPORATION **COULD** SET UP WAYS TO **CHECK** IT SO WHEN THE PRODUCT **GOES** TO THE CONSUMER IT SHOULD BE WHOLE, CLEAN AND **RIGHT**. BUT THEY'VE **LAID OFF** THE INSPECTORS 'CAUSE THEY DON'T **PRODUCE**, THEY ONLY **FIND** ERRORS, WHICH COSTS $ $.

MANAGEMENT WAS SHIP-PING **DEFEC-TIVE** PARTS AND SHOW ITEMS. **OUR** GUYS MADE RECORDS OF IT AND WE BAD-GERED THE INTERNATION-AL **UNION** TO **BLAST** THE HELL OUT OF GMAD.

THE BIGGEST POLLUTER IS THE THING WE PRODUCE, THE AUTOMOBILE. THE LIVELIHOOD THAT PUTS BREAD ON YOUR TABLE. I WOULDN'T WANT TO SEE ALL THE AUTOMOBILES BANNED BECAUSE THEY POLLUTE THE AIR. YET I REALIZE WHAT THE HELL GOOD IS MY LIVELIHOOD IF THE AIR'S GONNA KILL ME ANYWAY.

I THINK ALL THIS SMOG CONTROL IS TOKENISM, SIMPLY THAT. IT'S JUST ANOTHER GOSH DAMN GIMMICK. THEY'RE NOT REALLY FIGHTING AIR POLLUTION, THEY'RE NOT CONCERNED.

EVERY YEAR WE'VE HAD A POTENTIAL STRIKE ON OUR HANDS. IN SIX YEARS I'VE PUT OUT SIX STRIKE LETTERS. THERE ARE SO MANY THINGS TO DO. YOU MAJOR ON THE MINORS AND MINOR ON THE MAJORS. THAT MAJOR BEING POLLUTION, THE MINOR BEING OUR MONEY.

IN SOME PARTS OF THE PLANT CARS PASS A GUY AT 120 AN HOUR. THEY GOT ALL THE TECHNOLOGICAL IMPROVEMENTS. THEY GOT UNIMATES. BUT ONE THING WENT WRONG: THE HUMAN FACTOR. WE HAVE A SAY IN HOW HARD WE'RE GOING TO WORK. WE'RE PUTTING HUMAN BEFORE PROPERTY VALUE AND PROFITS.

WE'RE STILL MAKING 101 CARS AN HOUR, BUT NOW WE HAVE THE PEOPLE BACK GMAD LAID OFF. THEY TRIED TO CREATE A SPEED-UP BY USING LESS PEOPLE. WE STOPPED 'EM.

TEN TO TWELVE PERCENT OF OUR PEOPLE ARE BLACK OR HISPANIC. MOST OF THE SENIORITY PEOPLE ARE WHITES. THE BEST JOBS GO TO THE WHITE PEOPLE. TO ME, GENERAL MOTORS IS A BUNCH OF BIGOTS. THE OLDER GUYS STILL CALL EACH OTHER NIGGERS AND HONKIES.

THE YOUNG BLACK AND WHITE WORKERS DIG EACH OTHER. THERE'S AN UNDERSTANDING. THE GUY WITH THE AFRO, THE GUY WITH THE BEADS, THE GUY WITH THE GOATEE, HE DOESN'T CARE IF HE'S BLACK, WHITE, GREEN OR YELLOW.

OUR WOMEN HAVE BEEN HERE ONLY A YEAR. RIGHT NOW THEY'RE MORE INTERESTED IN LEARNING HOW THE UNION FUNCTIONS. I THINK WOMEN REALLY HELPED OUR UNION.

DRUGS ARE USED HERE. NOT SO MUCH HARD STUFF – THEY USE GRASS, SOME PILLS. THERE'S SOMETHING ELSE TO DRUGS. IT HAS TO DO WITH MONOTONY, WITH SOCIETY.

THE GUYS ARE NOT HAPPY HERE. THEY DON'T COME HOME THINKING: "BOY, I DID A GREAT JOB TODAY, AND I CAN'T WAIT TO GET BACK TOMORROW." I DON'T THINK HE THINKS A BLASTED THING ABOUT THE PLANT UNTIL HE COMES BACK.

THEIR IDEA IS NOT TO RUN THE PLANT. THEY JUST WANT TO BE TREATED WITH DIGNITY. THAT'S NOT ASKING A HELL OF A LOT.

I WEAVE IN ON BOTH SIDES OF THE ASSEMBLY LINE, TALKING TO GUYS. A LITTLE CONVERSATION. YOU DON'T WANT TO GET IN HIS WAY, 'CAUSE HE'LL RUIN A JOB.

AW, FUCK IT. IT'S ONLY A CAR.

IT'S MORE IMPORTANT TO JUST STAND THERE AND RAP.

I DON'T MEAN FOR CAR AFTER CAR.

IF SOMETHING'S LOOSE, OR DIDN'T GET INSTALLED, SOMEBODY'LL CATCH IT, SOMEBODY'LL REPAIR IT, HOPEFULLY. AT THAT POINT, HE MADE A DECISION: IT WAS JUST A LITTLE MORE IMPORTANT TO SAY WHAT HE HAD ON HIS MIND.

THE UNIMATE DOESN'T TALK, DOESN'T ARGUE, DOESN'T THINK. WITH US, IT BECOMES A HUMAN THING. IT'S THE MOST ENJOYABLE PART OF MY JOB, THAT MOMENT. I LOVE IT!

END

ADAPTED BY HARVEY PEKAR

ART BY RYAN INZANA

ELMER RUIZ

GRAVEDIGGER

Not anybody can be a grave—digger. You can dig a hole any—way they come. A gravedigger, you have to make a neat job. I had a fella that digged sewers. He was impressed when he saw me digg'n this grave, how square and perfect it was. A human body is going into this grave. That's why you need skill when you're gonna dig a grave.

He has dug graves for 8 years as an assistant to the foreman.

I used to cut grass and other things. I never had a dream to have this kind of job. I used to drive a trailer from Texas to Chicago.

He is married and has five children, ranging in age from 2 to 16.

It is a bitter, cold Sunday morning.

The gravedigger today,
they have to be somebody
to operate a machine.
You just use a shovel to
push the dirt loose.
Otherwise you don't use'em.
We're trying a new machine,
a GROUND HOG.
This machine is supposed
to go through heavy frost.
It do a very good job,
SO FAR.
When the weather is mild,
like 15° above zero,
you can do it very easy.

But when the weather is below zero, believe me, you just really work'n HARD. I have to use a mask. Your skin hurts when it's COLD-like you put a hot flame near your face. I'm talking about two, three hours standin' outside. You have to wear a mask, otherwise you can't stand it at all.

CHOK HOK   CHOK CH

Last year we had frost up to 35 inches deep, from the ground down. That was difficult to have a funeral. The frost and cement, it's about the same thing. I believe cement would break easier than frost. Cement is real solid, but when you hit'em, they CRACK. The frost, you just hit'em, they won't give up that easy.

CHOK CHOK

Last year we had to
use an AIR HAMMER
when we had 36 inches
of frost.

The most graves I dig is about 6, 7 a day. This is in the summer. In the winter it's a little difficult. In the winter you have 4 funerals. That's a pretty busy day. I been work'n kind of hard with this snow. We use CHARCOAL HEATERS. It's the same charcoal you use to barbecue ribs or hotdogs. I go and mark where the grave is gonna be tomorrow and put a layer of charcoal the same size of a box.

And this 15 inches of frost will be completely melted by tomorrow morning. I start early, about 7 o'clock in the morning, and have the park cleaned before the funeral. We have 2 funerals for tomorrow, 11 and 1 o'clock.

That's my life.

In the old days, it was supposed to be 4 men. 2 on each end with a rope, keep lower'n little by little. I imagine some fellas must weigh 200LBS. And I can feel the weight. We had a burial about 5 years ago, a fella that weighed 400LBS.

He didn't fit on the lower'n device. We had a big machine tractor that we could'a used, but that would'a looked kinda BAD, because lower'n a casket with a tractor is like lower'n anything. You have to RESPECT. We did it by hand. There were half a dozen men.

The grave will be covered in less than 2 minutes, COMPLETE.
We just open the hoppers with the right amount of earth. We just
press it and then we lay out a layer of black earth. Then we
put the sod that belongs there. After a couple of weeks you
wouldn't know it's a grave there. It's completely FLAT. Very rarely
you see a grave that's sunk. To dig a grave would take from
an hour to 45 minutes. Only 2 fellas do it. The operator of the
groundhog or backhoe and the other fella with the trailer where
we put the earth.

When the boss is gone I have
to take care of everything
MYSELF. That includes givin'
orders and so on. They make
it hard for me when the fellas
won't show. Like this new fella
we have. He's just great but
he's not dependable. He misses
A LOT. This fella, he's about 24
years old.

WHERE IS THAT GUY?

I usually tell 'em I'm a caretaker. I don't think that sounds so bad.
I have to look at the park, so after the day's over that everything's closed, that nobody do damage to the park.

WHUK

Some occasions some people just come and STEAL and LOOT and do
bad things in the park, destroy some things. I believe it would be
some young fellas. A man with RESPONSIBILITY, he wouldn't do
things like that. Finally we had to put up some gates and clos'em
at sundown. Before we didn't. No, we have a fence of roses. Always
188   in cars you can come.

WHEN YOU TELL PEOPLE YOU WORK IN A CEMETERY, DO THEY CHANGE THE SUBJECT?

Some they want to know. Especially Spanish people who come from Mexico. They ask me if it is true that when we bury somebody we dig'em out in 4, 5 years and replace them with another one I tell'em NO, HE'S BURIED FOR LIFE. It's a trade it's the same as a mechanic or a doctor.

You have to present your job correct—

—it's like an operation, if you don't know where to make the cut, you're not gonna have success. The same thing here. You have to have a little skill. I'm not talk'n COLLEGE or anything like that. Myself, I didn't have no grade-school, but you have to know what you're doing. You have some fellas been up for many years and still don't know whether they're com'n or goin'.

I feel proud when everything became smooth and when Mr. Bach congratulates us. 4 years ago, when the foreman had a heart attack, I took over, that was a real rough year for me. I had to dig graves and I had to show the fellas what to do.

MOVE IT OVER THERE.

A gravedigger is a very important person. You must have heard about the strike we had in New York about 2 years ago. There were 20,000 bodies lay'n and nobody could bury'em. The cost of funerals they raised and they didn't want to raise up the prices of the workers. The way they're livin', everything wanna go up and I don't know what's gonna happen.

LIVING WAGES

Y FOR

Believe we're not a rich people, but I think we livin fair.

We're not suffer'n. Like I know lots a people are having a rough time to live on this world because of the CRISES of the world.

My wife, sometimes she tired of stay'n here. I try to take her out as much as possible. Not to parties or clubs, but to stores and sometimes to drive-ins and so on.

She's used to funerals too. I gotta eat at noon and she asks me—

HOW MANY FUNERALS YOU GOT TODAY?

OH, WE BURIED 2.

HOW MANY MORE YOU GOT?

ANOTHER.

Some other people you go to your office, they say, "HOW MANY LETTERS YOU WRITE TODAY?" Mine says, "HOW MANY FUNERALS YOU HAD TODAY?"

My kids are used to everything. They start play'n ball right against the house. They're not authorized to go across the road, because it's the burial in there. Whenever a funeral gonna be across from the house, the kids are not permitted to play, one thing a kid love, like every kid is DOGS. In a way the dog in here would be the best thing to take care of the place. Especially a German Shepard. But they don't want dogs in here. It's not nice to see a dog around a funeral. Or cats or things like that.

I TOLD YOU, WE CAN'T HAVE A DOG ON ACCOUNTA MY JOB.

AAAWWWWW...!!

So they don't have no pet, no.

Can you imagine if I would'nt show up tomorrow morning and this other fella— he usually comes late— sometimes he don't show. We have a funeral for 11 o'clock, imagine what happens. The funeral arrives and where you gonna bury it? We put water, the aspirins in case somebody pass out. They have these capsules that you break and put up by their nose— SMELLING SALTS. And we put heaters inside the tents so the place be a little warm.

There are some funeral they REALLY affect you. Some young kids. We buried lot's of young. You have emotions you turn in, BELIEVE ME, you turn. I had a burial 2 years ago of teenagers, a young boy and a girl, this was real sad funeral because there was nobody but young teenagers.

I'm so used to going to funerals every-day—of course it bothers me—but I don't feel as bad as when I bury a young child. You really turn. I usually will wear myself some black sunglasses, it's a good idea because you EYES is the first thing that shows when you have a big emotion.

Always these black sunglasses.

The grief that I see everyday I'm really used to somebody's crying everyday, but there is some that are REAL BAD, when you just have to take it. Some people just don't want to give up. You have to understand that when somebody pass away, there's nothing you can do and you don't want to take it. If you DON'T take it, you're just gonna make your life WORSE, become SICK. People seems to take it more easier these days. They miss the person, but not as much.

There's some funerals that people, they show they're not SAD. This is different kinds of people. I believe they are happy to see this person—not in a way of singing-because this person is out of his suffer'n in this world. This person is gone and at rest for the rest of their life. I have this question lot's of times, "HOW CAN I TAKE IT?" They ask if I'm calm when I bury people. If you stop and think, a funeral is one of the natural things in the world.

When I finish my work here, I just don't remember my work. I like music so much that I have lots more time listen'n to music or play'n. That's where I spend my time. I don't drink. I don't smoke. I play Spanish bass and guitar. I play accordian. I would like to be a musician. I was born and raised in Texas and I never had a good school. I learned music myself from here and there. After I close the gate, I play.

THE END

About the Contributors

PABLO G. CALLEJO'S first book, *The Castaways*, written by Rob Vollmar, was an Eisner Award nominee. His second, *Bluesman* (also written by Vollmar), has been published in France, Spain, and the United States. He is currently working on *The Year of Loving Dangerously*, written by Ted Rall. He lives and works in Spain.

GARY DUMM, a Cleveland artist and frequent collaborator with Harvey Pekar, is the principal artist of *Students for a Democratic Society: A Graphic History*. His work has been published in the *New York Times*, *Entertainment Weekly*, and France's *Le Monde*, among many other places.

DANNY FINGEROTH spent many years as a writer and executive editor at Marvel Comics and is best known for his work on *Spider-Man*. He is also the author of several nonfiction prose works: *Superman on the Couch*; *Disguised as Clark Kent: Jews, Comics, and the Creation of the Superhero*; and *The Rough Guide to Graphic Novels*. He teaches comics at The New School and is a board member of the Institute for Comic Studies. He can be reached at: WriteNowDF@aol.com.

PETER GULLERUD worked for Warner Brothers for four years and Disney features for a decade, including visual development art for Aladdin. He is a self-taught artist and has been published by Fantagraphics, Graphic Classics, and other publishers, and he has just completed a four-hundred-page illustrated novel, *Fly with Wounded Wings*. He lives in Pine Mountain, California.

BOB HALL has drawn for Marvel, DC, and Valiant comics. He is remembered for his *Avengers* work at Marvel along with the graphic novel, *Emperor Doom*. At Valiant he wrote and drew *Shadowman* and *Armed and Dangerous*, while for DC he created *Batman* projects including *I, Joker*; *Batman DOA*, and *It's Jokertime*.

RYAN INZANA is an artist/author based in New Jersey. His graphic novel, *Johnny Jihad*, was ranked as one of *Booklist*'s top ten graphic novels of 2003. More of Ryan's work can be seen at his website, RyanInzana.com.

SABRINA JONES's *Isadora Duncan: A Graphic Biography* was published in 2008. A longtime editor of *World War 3 Illustrated*, she has created comics for *Wobblies! A Graphic History of the Industrial Workers of the World*, *The Real Cost of Prisons*, and *Mixed Signals*, a counterrecruitment tool in comic book form. She co-founded and edited *Girltalk*, an anthology of women's auto-biographical comics. Born in Philadelphia, she studied at Pratt Institute and the School of Visual Arts.

PETER KUPER grew up in Cleveland, where he met Harvey Pekar and a visiting Robert Crumb. He moved to New York in 1978 where he worked on *Richie Rich* comics and co-founded *World War 3 Illustrated* with Seth Tobocman, and since 1997 he has drawn the "Spy vs. Spy" feature for *Mad Magazine*. He lives in New York when he is not in Mexico.

In the 1990s, **TERRY LABAN** created the alternative comic book series *Unsupervised Existence*, *Cud*, and *Cud Comics*. He has worked as a writer for Egmont, Dark Horse Comics, and DC and is a political cartoonist and staff illustrator for the alternative monthly *In These Times*. *Edge City*, the daily comic strip he co-creates with his wife, Patty, was syndicated by King Features in 2001 and now appears in newspapers nation-wide. Find out more at www.labanarama.com.

DYLAN A.T. MINER is an assistant professor at Michigan State University, where he is core faculty in the Chicano/Latino and American Indian Studies programs. An art historian by training and an anarchist at heart, his work bridges indigenous and anticolonial knowledge with contemporary visual culture. Born and raised in rural Michigan, Dylan may be found crossing illegitimate borders with his partner and their two children. His visual and intellectual labor may be downloaded (free of charge) at dylanminer.com.

PAT MORIARITY is an award-winning cartoonist, illustrator, and animator who has collaborated on comics with Robert Crumb, Henry Rollins, and Harvey Pekar in his 1990s-era comic book *Big Mouth*. He's also created over seventy-five album covers, for musical acts like the Boss Martians, Charlie Burton, and the Von Zippers. His animation work has appeared in the acclaimed documentary *Derailroaded*. Visit www.patmoriarity.com

EMILY NEMENS hails from Seattle, Washington, and lives in Brooklyn. She has worked at the Smithsonian Institution's Archives of American Art and at the Metropolitan Museum in New York. She published a collection of short stories, *Scrub*, in 2007, wrote and illustrated a graphic novel about the 2004